Table of Contents

Title Page
Copyright
Front Matter
Table of Contents
Introduction
Understanding Minimalism
The Basics of Minimalist Living
How Minimalism Shapes Our Decisions
The Minimalist Mindset for Wealth
Adopting a Wealth-centric Minimalist Mindset
Shifting Perspectives Toward Financial Priorities
Decluttering Your Financial Life
Simplifying Financial Accounts
Eliminating Unnecessary Expenses
Intentional Spending
The Art of Mindful Purchases
Building Habits for Conscious Consumption
Setting Clear Financial Goals
Designing a Purposeful Financial Plan
Aligning Financial Goals with Life Values
Establishing a Budget That Works
Creating a Minimalist Budget
Maintaining Financial Discipline
Reducing Debt
Strategies for Rapid Debt Elimination
Navigating the Path to Financial Freedom
Saving with Purpose
Embracing a Simplistic Savings Strategy
Prioritizing Savings for Long-term Success
Investing the Minimalist Way
Investment Strategies for Simple Living
Diversification and Risk Management
Building Passive Income
Identifying Passive Income Opportunities
Sustaining Wealth Through Minimal Effort
Financial Independence
Planning for Early Retirement
Understanding the FIRE Movement
Practicing Gratitude and Contentment
Cultivating a Grateful Financial Perspective
Finding Fulfillment in Simplicity
Minimalist Living for Families
Raising Financially Savvy Children

- Creating a Family Budget Plan
- The Digital Minimalist Approach
- Utilizing Technology to Simplify Finances
- Managing Online Expenses Effectively
- Minimalist Travel
- Making Travel Affordable and Enjoyable
- Experiences Over Possessions
- Simplifying Your Home
- The Financial Benefits of Minimalist Spaces
- Reducing Home-related Expenses
- Sustainable Financial Practices
- Environmentally Conscious Financial Decisions
- Long-term Sustainability in Wealth Building
- Managing Economic Uncertainty
- Overcoming Financial Challenges
- Preparing for Economic Downturns
- The Role of Health and Wellness
- Financially Efficient Health Strategies
- Balancing Health and Wealth
- Time as a Financial Resource
- Maximizing Time for Financial Gain
- Time Management for a Minimalist Lifestyle
- Navigating Social Pressures
- Maintaining Minimalist Values in Social Settings
- Overcoming External Financial Expectations
- Leveraging Community and Relationships
- Building Financial Support Networks
- Sharing Resources and Knowledge
- Continuous Learning and Adaptation
- Staying Informed About Financial Trends
- Evolving Your Financial Strategy
- Reflecting and Reinventing
- Regular Financial Assessments
- Adapting Minimalism Over Time
- Leaving a Minimalist Legacy
- Planning for Generational Wealth
- Inspiring Others Through Your Financial Journey
- Conclusion
- Appendix

Minimalist Millionaire
The Art of Simple Wealth

by

David Holman

Copyright 2024 David Holman. All rights reserved.

No part of this book may be reproduced in any form or by any electronic or mechanical means including information storage and retrieval systems, without permission in writing from the author. The only exception is by a reviewer, who may quote short excerpts in a review.

Although the author and publisher have made every effort to ensure that the information in this book was correct at press time, the author and publisher do not assume and hereby disclaim any liability to any party for any loss, damage, or disruption caused by errors or omissions, whether such errors or omissions result from negligence, accident, or any other cause.

This publication is designed to provide accurate and authoritative information with regard to the subject matter covered. It is sold with the understanding that the publisher is not engaged in rendering professional services. If legal advice or other expert assistance is required, the services of a competent professional should be sought.

The fact that an organization or website is referred to in this work as a citation and/or a potential source of further information does not mean that the author or the publisher endorses the information the organization or website may provide or recommendations it may make.

Please remember that Internet websites listed in this work may have changed or disappeared between when this work was written and when it is read.

Minimalist Millionaire: The Art of Simple Wealth

Contents

Introduction
Chapter 1: Understanding Minimalism
- The Basics of Minimalist Living
- How Minimalism Shapes Our Decisions

Chapter 2: The Minimalist Mindset for Wealth
- Adopting a Wealth-centric Minimalist Mindset
- Shifting Perspectives Toward Financial Priorities

Chapter 3: Decluttering Your Financial Life
- Simplifying Financial Accounts
- Eliminating Unnecessary Expenses

Chapter 4: Intentional Spending
- The Art of Mindful Purchases
- Building Habits for Conscious Consumption

Chapter 5: Setting Clear Financial Goals
- Designing a Purposeful Financial Plan
- Aligning Financial Goals with Life Values

Chapter 6: Establishing a Budget That Works
- Creating a Minimalist Budget
- Maintaining Financial Discipline

Chapter 7: Reducing Debt
- Strategies for Rapid Debt Elimination
- Navigating the Path to Financial Freedom

Chapter 8: Saving with Purpose
- Embracing a Simplistic Savings Strategy
- Prioritizing Savings for Long-term Success

Chapter 9: Investing the Minimalist Way
- Investment Strategies for Simple Living
- Diversification and Risk Management

Chapter 10: Building Passive Income
- Identifying Passive Income Opportunities
- Sustaining Wealth Through Minimal Effort

Chapter 11: Financial Independence
- Planning for Early Retirement
- Understanding the FIRE Movement

Chapter 12: Practicing Gratitude and Contentment
- Cultivating a Grateful Financial Perspective
- Finding Fulfillment in Simplicity

Chapter 13: Minimalist Living for Families
- Raising Financially Savvy Children
- Creating a Family Budget Plan

Chapter 14: The Digital Minimalist Approach
- Utilizing Technology to Simplify Finances
- Managing Online Expenses Effectively

Chapter 15: Minimalist Travel
Making Travel Affordable and Enjoyable
Experiences Over Possessions
Chapter 16: Simplifying Your Home
The Financial Benefits of Minimalist Spaces
Reducing Home-related Expenses
Chapter 17: Sustainable Financial Practices
Environmentally Conscious Financial Decisions
Long-term Sustainability in Wealth Building
Chapter 18: Managing Economic Uncertainty
Overcoming Financial Challenges
Preparing for Economic Downturns
Chapter 19: The Role of Health and Wellness
Financially Efficient Health Strategies
Balancing Health and Wealth
Chapter 20: Time as a Financial Resource
Maximizing Time for Financial Gain
Time Management for a Minimalist Lifestyle
Chapter 21: Navigating Social Pressures
Maintaining Minimalist Values in Social Settings
Overcoming External Financial Expectations
Chapter 22: Leveraging Community and Relationships
Building Financial Support Networks
Sharing Resources and Knowledge
Chapter 23: Continuous Learning and Adaptation
Staying Informed About Financial Trends
Evolving Your Financial Strategy
Chapter 24: Reflecting and Reinventing
Regular Financial Assessments
Adapting Minimalism Over Time
Chapter 25: Leaving a Minimalist Legacy
Planning for Generational Wealth
Inspiring Others Through Your Financial Journey
Conclusion
Appendix A: Appendix

Introduction

In a world that often equates success with accumulation and prosperity with possession, the quest for financial freedom can feel like an uphill battle. Yet, beneath the bustling surface of our consumer-driven culture, a quieter revolution is gaining momentum. It's a movement that offers a fresh perspective on prosperity and challenges us to question the traditional metrics of wealth. Welcome to the world of minimalism, where less truly can be more, and where the path to financial freedom might not be about acquiring more but about intentionally living with less.

The idea of minimalism is not just about empty spaces and bare walls; it's about creating room for what truly matters. This concept can be a powerful tool in transforming our financial lives, steering us away from the endless desires that foster financial strain and towards a more deliberate approach to wealth. Minimalism invites us to strip away the excess, leaving behind a clear path to financial clarity and purpose.

As we embark on this journey, it's important to recognize that minimalism doesn't demand radical deprivation or a joyless existence. On the contrary, this approach aims to enhance your quality of life by aligning your financial habits with your personal values and aspirations. It's about setting the stage for a life that's not just rich in monetary terms but also abundant in meaning and satisfaction.

Consider this introduction your map to a financial journey where you redefine wealth, not just as a measure of money but also as a state of mind. The chapters ahead will guide you through a series of transformative steps: from understanding the fundamentals of minimalist living to adopting a wealth-centric mindset that prioritizes quality over quantity in financial decisions. You'll discover how to declutter your financial life, enabling you to channel your resources more effectively toward the goals that matter most.

Minimalism teaches us to realign our priorities, distinguishing between what is essential and what serves merely as a distraction. In financial terms, this means learning to distinguish between necessities and desires, between investments in the future and expenses that offer only momentary satisfaction. This book will empower you to simplify your financial landscape—streamlining accounts, eliminating superfluous expenses, and building a budget that genuinely works for you.

As you move forward, you'll explore how intentional spending and the art of mindful purchasing can liberate you from the cycle of consumerism, leading to profound benefits for your financial health. The minimalist approach encourages a shift in mindset, prompting you to buy less but choose more conscientiously. It's about constructing habits that support conscious consumption and recognizing that every purchase is a reflection of your life's priorities.

The journey to financial simplicity isn't just about spending less—it's about spending wisely and saving with a purpose. You'll learn how to develop a savings strategy that aligns with your long-term objectives, providing the financial security and peace of mind necessary to pursue your passions. Whether your goal is to retire early, travel more, or simply enjoy a stress-free retirement, the tools and strategies presented here are designed to guide you in prioritizing and building the foundation for enduring wealth.

Investing, often viewed as a complex and daunting task, is demystified through the lens of minimalism. By focusing on straightforward investment strategies that emphasize diversification and risk management, you'll be equipped to grow your wealth with confidence and clarity. This book will also introduce you to the concept of building passive income streams, offering you the chance to generate income with minimal effort and sustain your financial independence.

In this fast-paced world, where time is as valuable as currency, the minimalist philosophy also extends its wisdom to time management. By maximizing the time you have for financial gain and leveraging it as a crucial resource, you'll find that creating wealth isn't solely about the numbers—it's about the lifestyle you choose to lead and the legacy you intend to leave behind.

As you delve deeper into this exploration of financial minimalism, you'll realize that the journey extends beyond mere financial gain. It's about fostering a sense of gratitude and contentment with the simplicity of life, cultivating a mindset where abundance is measured not by accumulation but by happiness and fulfillment.

This book's roadmap is designed to be comprehensive, addressing various aspects of financial life that may apply differently depending on where you're starting from or where you wish to go. Whether you're single or managing a family budget, whether you aim for early retirement or just want to reduce financial stress, these chapters provide valuable insights and actionable advice tailored for a diverse audience.

The principles of minimalism can be applied to all facets of life, including your financial journey. This book serves as a beacon, illuminating a pathway through which you can achieve financial freedom with ease and purpose, all while minimizing unnecessary stress and maximizing the joys that come with a life of intentional simplicity.

Welcome to a new way of seeing and being, where simplicity and abundance coexist, and where financial wellness is more than just a goal—it's a way of life.

Chapter 1: Understanding Minimalism

In today's fast-paced world, minimalism stands as a beacon of simplicity and clarity. At its core, minimalism is about distilling life down to its essentials, focusing on what truly matters, and letting go of the rest. This philosophy isn't just about cleaning out your closet or living in a tiny house; it's about a mindset that can transform your approach to finances, relationships, and personal fulfillment.

Adopting a minimalist lifestyle starts with understanding your needs versus your wants. For many, life is cluttered with not just physical items but also financial commitments that don't serve their long-term well-being. By decluttering, we gain clarity. It's about freeing up mental and financial space to invest in experiences and goals that align with our values. When you embrace minimalism, you're not only paring down physical possessions but cutting through the noise of a consumer-driven society.

Minimalism asks us to question how we spend our time and money. Are our decisions driven by a desire for more, or are they based on genuine necessity and happiness? Take a moment to evaluate your surroundings and your bank statements. This reflection might initially feel daunting, but it is a powerful exercise in self-discovery. Gradually, as you sift through these layers, a newfound sense of purpose and direction emerges.

Our decisions, big or small, shape our lives. Minimalism encourages intentionality in each choice. By choosing less, we paradoxically gain more—more peace, more freedom, more satisfaction. What does your financial landscape look like when it's stripped back to basics? Imagine shedding the weight of financial obligations that don't enhance your life's quality and embracing a streamlined, purposeful approach.

Minimalism is not about deprivation; it is about liberation. It's an opportunity to pursue what brings real joy and fulfillment. By reducing distractions, we can concentrate on building wealth meaningfully. You pivot from living paycheck-to-paycheck to fortifying your financial future with deliberate, smart choices. Embrace minimalism, and watch it transform into a powerful ally in your pursuit of wealth and simplicity.

There's an authenticity that comes with minimalist living. It's a philosophy rooted in honesty—towards yourself and your aspirations. When every aspect of life, including your finances, aligns with minimalist principles, you find harmony. This seamless integration fosters an environment where financial growth is not just possible but inevitable.

The journey toward minimalism is deeply personal and uniquely yours. As you embark on this path, remember that it's not a race or a competition. It's an ongoing process of refining what minimalism means to you and how it best serves your journey towards financial freedom. Let this commitment to simplicity guide your way, bringing with it the riches of clarity and purpose.

The Basics of Minimalist Living

As we navigate the complexities of modern life, the concept of minimalist living offers a refreshing and impactful way to realign our priorities. Minimalism is more than just reducing physical clutter; it's about creating space for what truly matters. It invites us to thoughtfully assess our daily habits and encourages intentionality in how we spend our time, money, and energy.

At its core, minimalist living is guided by the principle of utility. Ask yourself, "Does this add value to my life?" If the answer isn't a resounding yes, consider cutting it out. This simple, yet profound question can revolutionize your daily decisions. By focusing on what you deem valuable, you cultivate a sense of fulfillment that transcends material possessions.

We live in a world bombarded with options, from the brands we wear to the cars we drive. Navigating through these choices can be daunting, often leading us to buy unnecessary items or make impulse decisions. Minimalism empowers you to sift through these distractions. It's like holding a magnifying lens to your life, homing in on what sparks joy and bringing it into sharper focus.

The journey toward minimalism begins with adopting an attitude of mindfulness. This means embracing deliberate decision-making and becoming aware of your consumption patterns. With mindfulness, each purchase transforms into a conscious transaction rather than an emotional response. This transition from reactive to proactive engagement with the world sets a foundation for financial freedom and peace of mind.

As you delve deeper into minimalist living, you'll notice shifts in how you define success and happiness. It's not about how much you own but appreciating what you have. By narrowing your focus to essentials, you allow yourself to appreciate each item, interaction, and activity that makes it past your newfound filter. This appreciation is the seedbed for contentment and simplicity—not just in finances but across all facets of life.

Our financial landscape is often cluttered with accounts, subscriptions, and debts that don't serve our goals. Embracing minimalist principles helps in cleaning up this clutter. Reduce multiple accounts and unneeded subscriptions, and watch as your financial picture becomes not only less overwhelming but also more coherent and manageable. You'll uncover unexpected sources of savings, too. Every little bit counts in creating a clearer path to achieving your financial dreams.

Minimalist living isn't simply about depriving yourself of pleasures or necessities. It's about making room for experiences that offer genuine satisfaction. When you spend less time and money chasing physical possessions, you free up time and resources for cherished experiences like travel, hobbies, and time spent with loved ones. This, in turn, fosters a deeper sense of happiness and well-being.

For some, embracing minimalism might mean owning fewer clothes, for others, it could translate to a digital detox. The beauty of minimalism lies in its flexibility and personal nature. It's not a one-size-fits-all model but a highly individual journey to define what 'enough' means to you. The concept encourages introspection and a gradual shedding of excess, leading you toward an existence where happiness isn't tied to material wealth.

Environmentally, minimalism can significantly reduce your ecological footprint. By owning less and opting for sustainable consumption, you participate in a movement aimed at conserving resources and promoting greater environmental consciousness. This not only benefits the planet but enriches your understanding of interconnectedness, emphasizing that every decision has a broader impact.

Of course, the path isn't always straightforward. As you adopt minimalist principles, you may face societal pressures to maintain a certain lifestyle or status. Remember, these pressures are often fleeting and shaped by external expectations. Staying true to minimalist values requires resilience and conviction. Holding steadfast to these values, however, brings peace unlike any societal measure of success could offer.

Minimalist living is an ongoing practice—a lifestyle choice that needs nurturing and refinement over time. As your circumstances evolve, so too might your interpretation of minimalism. Flexibility is key. Continual reassessment of goals and values ensures that you're living your most intentional and fulfilled life, at every stage.

Ultimately, minimalism prepares you for both present contentment and future prosperity. By streamlining your life in thoughtful ways, you unearth capacities to save, invest, and focus on long-term goals without the weight of material excess. As you weave minimalism into your financial decisions, you discover the profound joy in living simply, yet richly, in both spirit and wealth.

And so, as you stand at the threshold of minimalist living, be open to the transformations it may bring. Trust in its ability to cultivate a life of purpose and abundance, free from the entanglements of excess. Let it guide you to a future where clarity, intention, and fulfillment are the truest measures of wealth.

How Minimalism Shapes Our Decisions

Minimalism, at its core, invites a deeper engagement with the essence of what truly matters in our lives. This philosophy goes beyond decluttering our physical spaces; it extends into our decision-making processes, influencing the way we navigate our financial landscapes. Embracing minimalism requires a shift in mindset, prompting us to question not just what we own, but why we own it. It's about shedding the unnecessary to focus on what fuels our purpose.

At times, the multitude of choices we encounter can be overwhelming. As paradoxical as it may seem, having more options doesn't always equate to greater freedom or happiness. This is where minimalism lends its strength. By narrowing down choices to those that align with our core values and goals, we streamline decision-making. For instance, when deciding on a major purchase, a minimalist approach doesn't just assume 'Can I afford this?' but rather, 'Does this purchase align with my values and contribute to my goals?' This kind of thinking naturally fosters a more intentional allocation of our resources.

Connecting deeply with our intrinsic motivations helps us make decisions that reflect our true selves. Minimalism emphasizes authenticity and discourages the pursuit of superficial status symbols. As we internalize minimalist principles, we're less swayed by societal pressures and more inclined to trust our instincts. This self-awareness leads to more meaningful financial decisions. You learn to reject the unnecessary fillers that tempt your wallet — those impulse buys and fleeting trends — for choices that nurture long-term satisfaction and well-being.

Moreover, minimalism encourages living within our means, a practice that subtly shifts our financial focus from acquiring to managing what we already have. The habit of living minimally requires meticulous consideration of all expenses, forging a path to financial stability. It challenges us to justify each expenditure; frivolous purchases lose their allure, and what remains is a financial life built on intention and purpose.

By fostering clarity, minimalism ultimately empowers you to allocate funds in a manner that aligns closely with your broader life objectives. Through its lens, wealth is redefined — not as a collection of material goods, but as a collection of meaningful experiences, improved opportunities, and peace of mind. This redefined perspective prompts us to rethink how we invest our time as well, integrating our financial and personal well-being into one cohesive unit.

Minimalism also teaches us to value quality over quantity. In our consumer-driven world, the allure of abundance often overshadows our ability to appreciate the unique value of fewer, better possessions. Minimalism helps us reprioritize, steering decisions toward acquiring quality items that truly enhance our lives. This not only leads to more thoughtful spending but also reduces waste, aligning financial practices with sustainable values.

Consider this: Every financial transaction is an opportunity to vote for the kind of world you wish to live in. What does your spending say about your values? Are you supporting practices and industries that align with your vision of a better future? Minimalism encourages us to scrutinize these questions, to spend in ways that uphold our ideals, and to invest in change rather than complacency.

Another pivotal aspect of how minimalism shapes our decisions is by fostering adaptability. As our lives evolve, so do our needs and circumstances. Minimalism nurtures a mindset open to change, emphasizing flexibility and a readiness to adapt financial strategies as necessary. This adaptability is vital, not just in personal finance but in navigating ever-changing economic landscapes and financial uncertainties.

This approach also compels us to value experiences over possessions. A minimalist mindset encourages us to invest in moments that enrich our lives and deepen our connections with others. Financial decisions influenced by minimalism consider long-term fulfillment rather than short-lived excitement. This shift from accumulation to enrichment can transform our understanding of personal wealth.

Finally, at the heart of minimalist decision-making lies a sense of contentment and gratitude. By reducing the noise of excess and focusing on what truly matters, minimalism cultivates an appreciation for the present. Decisions made from a place of gratitude are often more grounded and fulfilling, providing a stable foundation for navigating financial choices with confidence and clarity.

In essence, a minimalist approach to decision-making is deeply personal and uniquely liberating. It asks us to delve beyond surface-level desires, encouraging choices that resonate with our deepest values and long-term aspirations. It invites us to curate our lives, shedding distractions to focus on what truly enhances our sense of purpose and fulfillment. By viewing decisions through a minimalist lens, we're not just simplifying our financial lives — we're crafting them with intention and meaning.

Chapter 2: The Minimalist Mindset for Wealth

Transitioning to a minimalist mindset offers profound benefits for those seeking financial freedom. It's more than just tidying up your space; it's about redefining what truly matters. Minimalism, when applied to finances, means stripping away the clutter to focus on what genuinely brings value and joy. This mindset encourages you to make deliberate choices that align with your personal and financial goals rather than succumbing to the chaos of consumer culture.

The journey towards adopting a minimalist approach begins with acknowledging the difference between needs and wants. While it's tempting to indulge in the allure of new gadgets or the latest fashion trends, minimalism teaches us the power of discernment. By prioritizing essentials, you not only save money but also unburden yourself from the unnecessary. Mindful spending becomes the cornerstone of financial minimalism, guiding you to channel resources towards things that truly enhance your life.

One of the remarkable aspects of embracing a minimalist mindset is how it reshapes your financial priorities. It's like putting on a different lens that sharpens your focus on long-term goals over fleeting pleasures. Suddenly, building an emergency fund or planning for retirement takes precedence over the allure of instant gratification. This shift doesn't require severe austerity but a thoughtful re-evaluation of how you allocate your resources to align with your deeper values.

A minimalist mindset also invites a reconsideration of success. Success isn't about accumulating more but achieving more with less. It's about experiences that create lasting memories rather than possessions that collect dust. It frees you to explore passions and hobbies, which often cost little but yield high returns in satisfaction. Investing in experiences, like learning a new skill or traveling, enriches your life in ways that possessions can't.

An understated but significant advantage of this mindset is the reduction of financial stress. When you declutter your financial affairs, you simplify decision-making, which leads to clarity and peace of mind. Consider the relief of knowing exactly where your money is going each month—there's understated power in this clarity. Minimalism imbues a sense of control over your finances, allowing for better planning and fewer financial surprises.

Moreover, the minimalist mindset fosters resilience. Financial challenges often come without warning, but minimalism builds a buffer by prioritizing savings and reducing liabilities. This not only equips you to handle downturns but also empowers you to seize opportunities when they arise. By living below your means, you create the flexibility needed to adapt and thrive amid economic uncertainty.

Minimalism isn't a one-size-fits-all approach. What works for one person may not suit another, and that's okay. The beauty lies in its adaptability—it can be tailored to fit your unique lifestyle and financial situation. It might mean downsizing to one car, simplifying meal plans, or even sharing resources with a community. The key is to find balance and ensure your financial decisions support your overall wellbeing.

As you embark on this journey, remember that minimalism isn't about deprivation. It's about intentionality. Each step taken towards this mindset positions you closer to financial liberation. With each unnecessary expense eliminated, you inch towards a goal that reflects a life of purpose and intention. Let this chapter be a catalyst, prompting you to reconsider how your choices can pave the path to a wealth of fulfillment and joy.

Adopting a Wealth-centric Minimalist Mindset
Embarking on the journey towards a wealth-centric minimalist mindset begins by redefining what prosperity truly means. It isn't about amassing more but about valuing what already exists in your life and freeing up resources to pursue what genuinely matters. This approach contrasts sharply with cultural narratives enamored with accumulation. By adopting this mindset, we shift focus from external symbols of wealth to the well-being and freedom that it can offer.

Minimalism, at its core, is about intent. When applied to wealth, it requires a deliberate exploration of how money influences our choices and lifestyle. The minimalist path isn't about deprivation; it's about mastery over our finances, ensuring that every dollar is intelligently purposed. This takes courage, a willingness to face financial truths, and the discipline to maintain core values while strategically pursuing financial goals.

A wealth-centric minimalist approach is intensely personal. Distilling financial priorities varies from person to person, intertwining with individual dreams and circumstances. For some, it means eliminating debts and financial obligations that stifle creativity and freedom. For others, it's an unwavering commitment to save or invest in experiences that bring genuine joy and growth. By aligning financial decisions with what truly enriches life, wealth becomes a tool for living with authenticity.

Through simplifying our financial lives, we release the emotional burden that complicated finances can carry. Complex financial landscapes, overloaded with accounts, debt, and unclear investments, blur our focus and drain energy. By clearing this clutter, we enhance our ability to make sound financial decisions that contribute to long-term prosperity. This process of simplification primes us for financial clarity and boosts confidence in our fiscal handling.

The minimalist mindset for wealth encourages an intrinsic review: Do our possessions serve our goals? In being mindful of the things we own, we also become mindful of how our spending reflects our deeper aspirations. This awareness nurtures intentional living and helps retain and build wealth, not by luck, but through informed choice and prudent stewardship.

A radical shift occurs when one focuses on the quality of life rather than the quantity of possessions. It opens possibilities for creativity and intelligence to fill the space that excess leaves behind. Financial management transitions from a burdensome duty to an empowering endeavor, where each decision is a step towards freedom. The slow but steady accumulation of savings or investments, when done with intent, compounds over time, securing a future where money isn't a constant source of stress or uncertainty.

Envisioning a future aligned with one's values requires discipline but promises rich rewards. Investing in this mental shift asks us to evaluate and challenge preconceived notions of necessity versus desire, luxury versus need. It's about reducing impulse spending and deciphering between transient wants and enduring satisfaction. By reigning in unwarranted expenditures, we discover that less can indeed be more.

The minimalist wealth mindset embraces adaptability and learning as vital elements. Financial landscapes shift, and flexibility in approaches ensures resilience and long-term success. As life's circumstances and priorities evolve, so should strategies for wealth.

Continuous learning instills confidence, while adaptability allows one to flow rather than fight against the tide of change.

Cultivating this mindset also frames wealth in the context of community and relationship-building. It prompts questions about how wealth can serve not only individual pursuits but communal benefit. The simple act of sharing knowledge or the resources we can spare elevates lives beyond our own and fosters a community where success is collective.

Lastly, adopting this approach involves understanding the significant role of contentment. Finding fulfillment in what one already has reduces relentless pursuit and competition. It allows gratitude to blossom, which paradoxically, tends to attract even more wealth—not just monetarily, but spiritually and emotionally. By embracing a wealth-centric minimalist mindset, we create a life where money exists to serve, not to rule.

In navigating this path, consider each action a deliberate choice towards greater freedom. As you do, remember that every step you take is a testament to living minimally but richly. This mindset holds the promise of not only financial independence but a fulfilling existence defined by clarity, purpose, and joyful abundance.

Shifting Perspectives Toward Financial Priorities

Stepping into the mindset of financial minimalism requires more than just decluttering our wallets; it demands a transformation in how we view and prioritize our financial obligations. This shift isn't about deprivation or sacrifice; it's about recognizing the abundance that lies in simplicity and intention. When we realign our financial priorities, we are not just budgeting better, but we are aligning our spending with our deepest values and desires.

Consider the dynamic of wants versus needs. It's a conversation as old as consumer culture itself, yet remains a crucial starting point for financial realignment. Needs are the essentials—food, housing, and healthcare—while wants are those extras that adorn our lives. Minimalism encourages us to break free from societal benchmarks of success and redefine what is truly essential for our happiness and well-being. It's about discerning the hidden costs and striving for purchases that enlarge our life, not our liabilities.

As we journey through this transformative process, it's important to understand that financial minimalism doesn't equate to owning less of everything; rather, it emphasizes owning more of the right things. It's acknowledging that money is a tool that can be wielded to forge a life of freedom rather than just means to accumulate stuff. The essence lies not in abstinence but in choosing with intention, sharpening our focus on the quality of our purchases rather than their quantity.

Navigating this shift also involves embracing experiences over possessions. The memories we create hold intrinsic value that no material possession can replicate. These enrich our lives in countless ways, offering returns in personal growth and fulfillment that cannot be measured by the dollar. By prioritizing experiences, we cultivate a life that is both abundant and uncluttered, filled with valuable connections and moments rather than objects.

Financial priorities often demand us to step back and ask critical questions: What truly brings joy? What further enriches our journey? Answering these questions honestly can unveil surprising insights. It may reveal how much energy has been funneled into maintaining a lifestyle that doesn't resonate with our genuine aspirations. By reassessing priorities, we choose alignment with passion and purpose over keeping up appearances.

In this quest for financial perspective, cultivating gratitude plays an instrumental role. Adopting a mindset of thankfulness for what we currently possess reorients our focus away from scarcity. This transforms how we allocate not just our money but our attention and energy. When we appreciate the simplicity of what we have, we naturally spend less effort chasing what we don't. Gratefulness isn't merely a passive sentiment but an active practice that reshapes our entire approach to finances.

Embracing change might feel daunting, but it unfolds new horizons for growth. Many find that as they shift perspectives, they let go of the fear that accompanies financial decisions. This newfound understanding frees them to invest their hard-earned dollars in ways that resonate deeply with their personal values. It's an empowering transition from a consumer-driven existence to one enriched by authentic choices and genuine fulfillment. Furthermore, by realigning our financial priorities, we create more space—both physically and mentally—allowing for clearer, more intentional living. This clarity makes it easier for us to discern opportunities for saving and investing, paving the way for a financially secure future. As we strip away the superfluous, our relationship with money transforms: we become its master rather than its servant.

Community and relationships also experience a profound impact as we shift financial perspectives. Instead of viewing social interactions as costly endeavors, they become opportunities to share resources, knowledge, and support. This collaborative approach fosters a sense of belonging and collective growth, reminding us that wealth is not the possession of financial assets alone but the strength and depth of our connections. Ultimately, shifting perspectives toward financial priorities empowers us to live in alignment with what matters most. It's a path that leads not just to financial security but to lives rich with purpose and gratitude. This journey towards minimalism doesn't happen overnight but unfolds gradually, requiring patience and persistence. Through this conscious shift, we're one step closer to not just surviving, but truly thriving in our financial lives.

Chapter 3: Decluttering Your Financial Life

When it comes to finances, clutter doesn't just fill our spaces—it fills our minds. We live in a world that often pushes us to accumulate more than we need, whether that be extra accounts, subscriptions, or even insurance policies. But by streamlining these aspects, you create space not just in your wallet, but also in your mind. It begins with a willing heart and a clear intention to break free from the unnecessary.

The first step in decluttering your financial life involves taking a good, hard look at your financial accounts. Do you really need both a checking and multiple savings accounts, each tied to different banks? Or might it be simpler to consolidate? Simplifying these accounts can relieve the stress of managing multiple passwords, balancing numerous statements, and worrying about various fees. In today's digital age, many banks offer seamless services that cater to minimalist ideals—you'd be surprised how much lighter you'll feel once you've let go of the excess.

Let's also consider those recurring expenses that sneak up and rob you of your hard-earned money. Old gym memberships or subscriptions you no longer use should be the first to go. Going through your monthly statements might seem daunting at first, but every unnecessary charge eliminated is one less chain holding you down. When you allocate your funds toward what truly matters, you cultivate both financial independence and well-being.

Finally, remember that decluttering isn't about learning to live with less for the sake of deprivation. It's about focusing on what adds value to your life. It's about aligning your spending with your deepest values and removing the financial noise. When you let go of what no longer serves you, you make room for growth, allowing your wealth to build steadily and intentionally. Your journey to financial freedom starts with simplicity, and from simplicity springs opportunity.

Simplifying Financial Accounts

In a world filled with complex financial products and services, one might easily become overwhelmed by the sheer number of accounts society compels us to maintain. Bank accounts, credit cards, retirement funds, and more—all demanding attention and inducing stress. Simplifying your financial accounts isn't just about tidying up; it's a crucial step towards a less stressful and more intentional financial life.

First, let's consider the primary accounts necessary for a streamlined financial life. While not everyone has the same needs, most individuals will benefit from having a simple set-up: a checking account for everyday expenses, a savings account for emergency funds, and one or two retirement accounts for long-term growth. Anything beyond these basics should be scrutinized. Ask yourself, does it serve a specific purpose that aligns with your financial goals?

The act of maintaining numerous accounts not only creates clutter but also fogs our financial vision. When you have accounts scattered across various institutions, it's easy to lose track of where your money is going and how it's growing. Consolidating accounts where possible provides clarity and enhances your ability to manage your finances effectively. By having fewer accounts, you allow yourself the luxury of a comprehensive view, which is fundamental for making informed financial decisions.

Now, let's tackle the emotional aspect. Yes, emotions play a substantial role in our financial decisions. We often accumulate financial products over time, each tied to a different life phase or attempt at security. Consequently, we end up holding on to them due to a sense of familiarity or a fear of letting go. However, it's important to remember that these accounts aren't serving you if they're not contributing to your current or future financial well-being. When simplifying your accounts, use this opportunity to cancel those that no longer align with your financial objectives. Often, this means closing redundant bank accounts that don't offer any unique benefits. Similarly, if you have multiple credit cards, you should evaluate which ones to keep based on their perks and your spending habits. Simplification doesn't mean deprivation; rather, it's about letting go of what doesn't add value so that you can focus on what truly does.

Some people keep multiple retirement accounts from various jobs or old employers. Rolling these into a single account often simplifies management and might also reduce fees. Consolidation into an IRA or a single 401(k) can be a good strategy for reducing complexity, making it easier to monitor growth and adjust strategies as needed. Always ensure that consolidation makes sense for fees, investment options, and your overall retirement strategy.

Bank fees and minimum balance requirements are another consideration when simplifying accounts. Many accounts come with hidden costs that, over time, erode your financial health. By eliminating unnecessary accounts, you can also break free from these financial shackles. Focus your efforts on accounts that offer low fees and favorable terms that are aligned with your needs. These should support your financial habits and goals, not hinder them.

Let's not overlook the importance of digital tools in simplifying financial accounts. Today, numerous apps and platforms can help manage your finances more efficiently. However, be cautious; just because a tool is available doesn't mean it's necessary. Select a few key applications that sync with your accounts for budgeting, tracking, and forecasting purposes. Too many tools can lead to the same problem as too many accounts—information overload and fragmented oversight.

After streamlining, regularly review your accounts to ensure they still meet your needs. Financial simplification isn't a one-time event but a continual process. Life circumstances change, and so might the accounts best suited to handle them. By periodically assessing your financial situation, you stay proactive, keeping your financial life aligned with your aspirations and priorities.

Finally, remember that a minimalist approach to financial accounts is not an end, but a means to achieving greater financial freedom. With fewer accounts come greater focus, a clearer mind, and the capacity to direct your energy towards building wealth intentionally. This simplicity allows for a deeper engagement with your financial life, ensuring that every decision you make is well thought out, empowering, and aligns with your long-term vision.

Simplifying financial accounts is a powerful move towards reducing stress and increasing control over your financial destiny. Through thoughtful evaluation and strategic reduction, you can pave the way for a financial life that supports the journey to freedom. It is an essential element in the art of living minimally and mindfully, a cornerstone in building a life centered on what's truly important.

Eliminating Unnecessary Expenses

In the pursuit of financial freedom through a minimalist lens, one of the core principles is learning to recognize what truly matters. This means ruthlessly eliminating expenses that don't serve your essential needs or long-term goals. Simplification isn't just about reducing clutter in your physical space; it extends to every dollar you spend. Imagine your finances as a garden. Just as a gardener removes weeds to give more space and nutrients to the thriving plants, you must prune unnecessary expenses to nourish your financial growth. Let's start by identifying these unnecessary expenses, a step that requires honesty and courage. We often hide behind convenience and habit, opting for quick solutions rather than questioning the actual value of our purchases. Many everyday expenses masquerade as needs when they are merely comforts. It's time to challenge these assumptions. Begin with your regular bills, subscriptions, and memberships. Are you paying for a gym you rarely visit, or subscribing to a streaming service you no longer use? Small expenses can accumulate like dust, gradually dulling your financial shine.

Another key area to examine is your spending on non-essential luxury items. While there's no harm in treating yourself occasionally, these should be intentional choices, not default behaviors. Ask yourself if the joy derived from such purchases outlives the swipe of your card. Often, we buy things not out of necessity but because they promise momentary happiness or status. Minimalism in finance asks us to align spending with values, ensuring that purchases enhance our lives rather than clutter them.

Grocery bills provide a practical example of unnecessary expenses that can be streamlined. The first step is adopting meal planning, which cuts down waste and encourages home-cooked meals, contributing to healthier eating habits and helping control excess spending. Bulk buying can save money, but only when it aligns with actual consumption patterns. Here, the lessons of simplicity and intention come full circle: buy only what you will use, and use what you buy. This approach not only benefits your pocket but respects resources, fostering a sustainable lifestyle.

Transportation is another area ripe for reconsideration. Car payments, insurance, and maintenance contribute significantly to monthly outgoings. Many find value in evaluating public transportation options, carpooling, or biking, which are often healthier and more affordable alternatives. If you've two cars in the household, contemplate the possibility of managing with just one. Though this change demands initial adjustments, it can result in substantial savings that bolster your financial stability.

As you sift through expenditures, automate what you can pay without delay and track what needs attention. Consider using budgeting apps to categorize expenses, highlighting patterns that might show areas for reduction. Set alerts for payment deadlines to avoid late fees, and analyze credit card statements, which often reveal obscure subscriptions or erroneous charges.

In a culture that equates more with better, it's vital to recognize the allure of consumerism. Eliminating unnecessary expenses often means turning down offers, refusing upgrades, and saying no to limited-time offers. Sales and discounts can create a sense of urgency, pressuring us into making decisions that deviate from our core values and priorities. Practicing patience allows for thoughtful decision-making—wait a day, a week, or a month before making a purchase that's not essential, and observe whether the need persists.

Technology, in many ways, can simplify this process. Use digital tools to unsubscribe from marketing emails, enabling strategic shopping rather than impulse buying. Streamline your phone apps and web services to suit real needs, possibly transitioning to lower-cost alternatives for services you do wish to retain. Setting boundaries in your digital life can lessen the interruption of noise, allowing you to focus on what truly matters, both financially and personally.

While it's tempting to focus on cutting expenses alone, it's equally important to redirect the saved funds. Consider allocating them to an emergency fund or using them to accelerate debt repayment, both of which build financial stability. This savings expansion reinforces the idea that eliminating unnecessary expenses is not about deprivation but strategic reallocation towards robust financial health.

People are often concerned that giving up expenditures equates to sacrificing quality of life. However, minimalism teaches us that quality is not reflected by the digit on a price tag but by the richness of experiences and peace of mind. Life enriched by genuine engagements, be it in community activities, nature walks, or home-cooked family dinners, holds more value. The joy derived from relationships and experiences often outweighs material possessions.

Scientific studies suggest that beyond a certain point, additional income brings diminishing returns on happiness. Once basic needs and some comforts are met, the pursuit of more can lead to stress and dissatisfaction. Embracing minimalism encourages you to identify this "enough" point, subtracting distractions so the finances align with what truly enhances your life.

In essence, eliminating unnecessary expenses is not just a calculated move to cut costs but a profound shift towards conscious living. It's about creating space not merely in a budget sheet but within life itself, granting the freedom to live more intentionally. This change is a step closer to the overarching goal of financial freedom through simple and meaningful living.

Chapter 4: Intentional Spending

As we venture into the realm of intentional spending, let's unearth its profound impact on our financial journey. Embracing intentionality isn't just a financial strategy; it's a lifestyle choice that aligns your spending with your values. Every dollar spent becomes a decision that reflects what's truly important. But how do we step into this mindful approach?

Begin with awareness. Take a moment to consider your recent purchases—were they impulsive or deliberate? Mindful spending requires us to pause and evaluate our motives before making transactions. It's about questioning needs versus wants, understanding the emotional triggers that lead to spur-of-the-moment purchases, and putting a stop to them. This doesn't mean we should deny ourselves pleasures, but rather prioritize joy over fleeting satisfaction. The beauty of intentional spending lies in its power to bring clarity and purpose to our financial behaviors.

To cultivate intentional habits, create systems that support conscious consumption. This could mean setting up alerts to remind you of saving goals or reminders before purchasing items. Imagine transforming routines not into rigid rules but into flexible frameworks that guide financial choices. Such frameworks allow for both discipline and spontaneity, giving freedom to decide without guilt.

Intentional spending also leads us to rethink our relationship with material goods. Investing in experiences rather than things can enrich our lives without cluttering our space. Experiences shape who we are—they are stories we tell and memories we cherish. Consider the value in exploring new places, learning new skills, or spending quality time with loved ones. The fulfillment and growth gleaned from these are priceless.

Ultimately, intentional spending is about aligning every expenditure with a greater purpose. It's a commitment to living in harmony with our financial goals and personal values. With every step in this direction, we not only reclaim control over our resources but also transform our financial landscape into one of prosperity and contentment.

The Art of Mindful Purchases

Intentional spending begins with understanding the art of mindful purchases. In a world where consumer messages bombard us at every turn, it's easy to get swept away in the tide of instant gratification. But if you're aiming for financial freedom through intentional living, buying with mindfulness is key.

Let's start with a simple truth: every purchase is a choice. This seemingly obvious idea holds immense power. By acknowledging that you're in control of what, when, and why you buy, you shift the narrative from one of passive consumption to active decision-making. The goal isn't just to buy less; it's to buy better, to invest in what truly enriches your life, rather than what clutters it.

Consider the story of a well-worn leather journal. Every scratch and faded page tells a tale of moments captured, thoughts penned, and dreams mapped out. Unlike a stack of unused notebooks bought on a whim, this one item holds value beyond its price. It embodies the idea that mindful purchases are those that consistently provide value, utility, and even beauty.

To master mindful purchasing, begin with introspection. Ask yourself: What drives your spending habits? Is it a desire to impress, a response to boredom, or maybe a quest for fleeting happiness? Understanding the underlying motivations can illuminate patterns that need reshaping. Once you identify these patterns, you can strategize to counter them with intentionality.

Next, cultivate awareness by tapping into your sensory experiences. Before making a purchase, pause to assess how it makes you feel. Does the idea of owning the item bring genuine joy, or is it a temporary thrill? Visualize how the item fits into your life, not just your home. In doing so, you begin to tie your buying choices to your broader values and goals.

There's also a technique known as the "wait before you buy" rule. It involves delaying purchasing decisions for a specific period, say 30 days, particularly for items that aren't necessities. This pause gives you time to genuinely evaluate the purchase's importance, which often results in reconsideration, especially when emotions cool. It's a simple yet effective way to combat impulse buying.

Moreover, embrace a shift from quantity to quality. Choose fewer items that are well-made, ethically produced, and add real value to your life. Consider these items as investments in your lifestyle rather than mere additions to your inventory. For instance, a high-quality kitchen tool can enhance your culinary endeavors and last for years, transforming cooking from a chore to a cherished hobby.

While we're on the subject of quality, let's not overlook the importance of community and storytelling in purchases. Items with a story, whether handcrafted by local artisans or purchased during travels, often carry meaning beyond their material presence. By supporting sustainable businesses or buying locally, you contribute to a positive feedback loop that aligns with intentional living.

Mindful purchases also involve a conscious interaction with marketing. Today's advertising landscape is clever, crafting campaigns to make you believe you need something you don't. Cutting through the noise requires a critical eye—questioning the authenticity and necessity of what's being sold to you.

Building a checklist can further streamline the process. Before any purchase, mentally—or physically—check if the item meets essential criteria: Do you truly need it? Does it align with your values? Does it offer long-term satisfaction? This checklist acts as a safeguard, filtering out potential clutter and promoting clarity.

Equally, reflecting on past purchases can offer valuable insights. Evaluate purchases that brought lasting joy versus those that didn't. Why do some items resonate more with your life? Use these reflections to guide your future buying decisions.

Conscious consumption extends beyond the initial purchase. Responsible stewardship of your possessions is essential. Rather than disposing of items recklessly, find ways to prolong their life through maintenance, repurposing, or selling. It builds a satisfying cycle of use that upholds your intentional living values.

Ultimately, the art of mindful purchases helps you cultivate a financial life that echoes simplicity and purpose. Each careful decision acts as a stitch in the fabric of a lifestyle that prioritizes meaningful engagement with material goods over empty accumulation. Through this practice, you not only gain financial clarity but also see that true freedom is less about owning more and more about cherishing the right things.

As you refine your purchasing habits, remember that change doesn't happen overnight. It requires a gentle persistence—a commitment to align your actions with your aspirations. Mindful purchases are about awareness, deliberation, and alignment with your true self, leading you step by step towards a more intentional, financially liberated life.

Building Habits for Conscious Consumption

Building habits for conscious consumption is like learning a new language. At first, it feels foreign, but with practice, it becomes second nature. It's about making purchasing decisions that align with your values and financial goals, reducing excess, and focusing on what truly matters to you. It can seem daunting, but remember, like any worthwhile pursuit, it starts with a single step—a commitment to change.

Think of conscious consumption as a mindfulness exercise for your finances. It involves actively considering the implications of each purchase. When faced with a potential buy, ask yourself: "Does this align with my long-term goals? Am I buying this to fill an emotional void or satisfy a passing whim?" By being honest with yourself, you begin to build a habit of pausing and reflecting, creating space for intentional decisions rather than impulsive ones.

Begin with small, manageable changes. Start by identifying areas in your life where spending feels excessive or mindless. It could be your morning coffee routine, your subscription services, or even your dining-out habits. It's not about deprivation but rather re-evaluating and redirecting resources to places that bring lasting value and joy. By choosing to brew your coffee at home or retaining just those subscriptions that you truly need, you're not just saving money; you're reclaiming a sense of control.

A practical tool in fostering conscious consumption is keeping a spending journal. Record each purchase and reflect on its necessity and emotional impact. Over time, patterns emerge—patterns that can guide future decisions. While occasionally indulging in a non-essential item isn't verboten, the journal helps balance these decisions against your larger financial picture. It's about cultivating awareness and learning from each choice rather than mindlessly following the routine.

If you're married or share finances with a partner, conscious consumption becomes a joint exercise in communication and alignment. Discuss your shared financial dreams and aspirations. Practice the art of compromise when deciding what's worth spending on and what isn't. This open dialogue fosters mutual understanding and strengthens both the relationship and your financial position by aligning on what truly adds value to your shared life.

Amidst daily life, we sometimes overlook the power of gratitude in reshaping spending habits. Regularly practicing gratitude shifts attention away from what you lack and toward appreciation for what you already have. This mindset can significantly impact consumption choices. It's less about acquiring new things and more about cherishing current blessings, adding layers of satisfaction that purchases might fail to deliver.

Now, diversifying your experiences rather than expanding your belongings opens up a new avenue toward conscious consumption. Experiences such as a hike with friends or a day spent exploring your city can offer more profound satisfaction than accumulating physical goods. As you replace buying with being, you slowly transform the urge to acquire into the joy of experiencing.

Remember, perfection isn't the goal. Life is full of unexpected turns, and rigid rules can lead to unnecessary stress. The intention is to build a flexible yet disciplined approach to spending. Each conscious decision is a learning moment that propels you further along your financial journey, teaching you more about your needs, desires, and the underlying motivations driving them.

Ultimately, building habits for conscious consumption is deeply personal and transformative. It's a journey toward financial freedom, guided by choices that reflect who you are and hope to become. Embrace this shift toward a life rich in meaning, not just in material possessions. As these habits take root, they'll naturally guide you toward a simpler, more intentional lifestyle, propelling you closer to your ultimate goal of financial freedom.

Chapter 5: Setting Clear Financial Goals

Setting clear financial goals is like plotting a course on a map. It provides direction and purpose, guiding you toward a life aligned with your deepest values. Before we can move forward with a plan, it's crucial that your goals reflect what genuinely matters to you. Maybe it's retiring early, traveling the world, or something as simple as stress-free living. The key is to dig into your personal values, unearthing what truly brings you joy and satisfaction. Once discovered, these values become the foundation upon which your financial goals stand.

Now, let's talk about the structure. Your goals need to be specific, measurable, achievable, relevant, and time-bound—yes, the good old SMART goals. Instead of just saying, "I want to save money," try defining a clear target like, "I aim to save $10,000 for an emergency fund within the next 18 months." This specificity transforms a wishful thought into a clear objective, motivating you as you track progress along the way.

Goal alignment with life values not only simplifies your approach but also injects meaningful intent into every dollar spent or saved. Re-evaluating these goals regularly is essential, too, ensuring they continue to reflect your evolving life circumstances and aspirations. Life changes, and so should your goals. This consistent recalibration helps maintain the momentum and keeps your financial journey vibrant and aligned.

Keep in mind, the journey to financial clarity demands both courage and adaptability. Sometimes, this means letting go of societal pressures and expectations to pursue what feels right for you. And this journey isn't just about financial gain but about creating a life that's rich in experiences and personal fulfillment. With clear goals set, you're well on your path to simplifying your financial life and, importantly, growing your wealth in meaningful ways.

Designing a Purposeful Financial Plan

Crafting a financial plan that truly resonates with your life goals is both an art and a science. It requires not just the mind, but also the heart. When embarking on this journey, imagine what it feels like to be guided by values and intentions rather than merely numbers. The beauty of a purposeful financial plan lies in its power to bridge your dreams and reality, turning hypothetical aspirations into achievable milestones.

A purposeful financial plan starts with clarity. To know where you're heading, first, you must understand where you stand. Begin by taking a thorough inventory of your current financial situation. This means tallying up assets, liabilities, income, and expenses. Clarity isn't just in the numbers, though—it's in articulating your desires and recognizing the values that drive those desires. It's about making sure your money serves your life, not the other way around.

Next comes setting priorities. Life is filled with choices and trade-offs. In a world that often tells us to want more, need more, and consume more, deciding what's truly important to you may involve peeling back layers of societal expectations. Ask yourself: What do you want most in life? What energizes you and fills you with joy? These questions anchor the financial decisions that follow. Whether it's a dream of owning a home, funding education, or retiring in comfort, your financial priorities should clearly reflect your personal values.

Once priorities are clear, the path to weaving them into a plan involves setting intentional financial goals. Goals are the tangible representation of your intentions. They need to be specific and measurable to provide direction, achievable to maintain motivation, relevant to stay aligned with your values, and time-bound to create urgency and a timeline for achievement. Consider adopting the SMART criteria to ensure your goals are well-structured and attainable.

Moreover, every financial decision should be evaluated through the lens of these goals. For instance, if one of your goals is to travel more extensively, consider how your daily expenses align or conflict with saving for these adventures. It might mean dining out less frequently or cutting back on unnecessary subscriptions—choices that can free up funds for what truly matters to you.

A solid financial plan, however, is not a rigid set of rules; it's a living, breathing document that evolves as your circumstances, desires, and values change. It requires regular reflection and adjustment. Life is unpredictable, and so a degree of flexibility is not just prudent, but necessary. Your plan should account for change—whether that's a shift in personal priorities or an unexpected life event.

In this way, designing a purposeful financial plan is akin to tending a garden. It demands attention, care, and a willingness to prune and nurture as needed. There will be seasons of growth and times of patience, but the intention behind each action guides the plan's development. Reflecting on progress, celebrating small wins, and resetting when goals are met or changed keeps the journey enriching.

Mitigating risks is another cornerstone of your financial blueprint. While ambition drives goals forward, a healthy respect for life's uncertainties ensures resilience. Building an emergency fund, considering insurance, and planning for financial downturns are strategies to safeguard against unexpected disruptions. It's about maintaining a cushion that allows you to stay on course despite potential roadblocks.

As you craft your financial plan with purpose and intention, remember that this journey is as much about self-discovery as it is about financial success. Embrace the process of uncovering what truly brings you fulfillment. This approach can transform how you view money—not as an end, but as a means to a more intentional way of living.

Ultimately, your financial plan should feel inspiring, even exciting. It's not just a roadmap, but a source of motivation and empowerment. Aligning your finances with your deepest values invites a sense of control and meaning into your life. You're not just planning for goals in isolation; you're orchestrating a narrative of financial freedom intertwined with personal satisfaction.

Your purposeful financial plan is ready to be your compass—helping you navigate the complexities of life with clarity, confidence, and peace of mind. Embrace the simplicity in knowing that with each thoughtful financial decision, you're crafting a life that stays true to who you are. In the process, you're not just building wealth; you're building a future that truly resonates with your core values.

Aligning Financial Goals with Life Values

In today's fast-paced world, aligning financial goals with your core life values is like finding a true north amid countless distractions. It's easy to get caught up in society's expectations, pursuing goals that don't resonate with who we are at our core. When we align our financial aspirations with our personal values, we're not just moving numbers around. We're shaping the kind of life we want to lead. One that brings every aspect of our existence into harmony. This alignment is the bridge between what we earn and how we choose to spend or save, transforming mundane financial planning into a meaningful life journey.

Financial freedom is not just about having ample resources to do as you please. It's about understanding what truly matters to you, then using your financial resources to support those essential values. This could mean prioritizing education, family time, adventure, or perhaps sustainability and community engagement. By placing values at the forefront of financial planning, investments and spending become reflections of personal beliefs, fostering a deep sense of peace and satisfaction.

To begin this alignment, start by identifying your core values. Ask yourself: What activities or causes ignite passion? What kind of legacy do you wish to leave? Contemplate what success looks like to you, not just in financial terms but as a holistic measure of well-being and fulfillment. This introspection might take time and might change over different life stages, but it's foundational to setting goals that matter.

Once your values are clear, the next step is to set financial goals that reflect those values. Let's say sustainability is high on your list. You might aim to invest in green energy projects or commit to reducing the carbon footprint of your household. If family and relationships top your list, your financial goals might focus on allocating resources toward creating memorable experiences together or supporting relatives in need. Here, financial strategies become a means to an end rather than the end itself.

As you embark on aligning financial goals with life values, remember that this is a dynamic process. Life is unpredictable, and as circumstances and priorities change, so too may your financial goals. Regular reflection is crucial. By habitually revisiting your goals and values, you ensure that your financial path remains relevant and meaningful, allowing for growth and change.

Practical tools like vision boards or value charts can help visualize this alignment. Seeing them laid out on paper or digital format helps solidify them in your mind, making them easier to manifest in your day-to-day activities. Similarly, journaling about financial decisions and their alignment with your values can provide perspective. This introspective practice can lead to greater diligence and joy in the financial goal-setting process.

The process of aligning financial goals with life values is one of liberation. It frees you from the constraints of arbitrary financial pursuits determined by external pressures. Instead, it allows for a deep sense of control and intentionality over finances. When every expenditure, investment, and saving decision aligns with personal values, there's a feeling of congruence between financial actions and inner beliefs that's profoundly satisfying.

Ultimately, aligning financial goals with life values cultivates not just wealth, but a richer, more meaningful life. It's an approach that embraces the intricate tapestry of our desires, dreams, and beliefs, forging a path that's uniquely ours. This radical alignment empowers us to lead lives of intentionality, leaving us not only financially stable but enriched with purpose and contentment.

Chapter 6: Establishing a Budget That Works

Creating a budget isn't just about numbers; it's about crafting a lifestyle that supports your dreams and values. A successful budget is a dynamic tool guiding you toward your financial aspirations, not a set of constraints trapping you. As you begin this journey, remember that your budget should reflect your unique priorities and be adaptable to the ebbs and flows of life. This flexibility ensures that it remains relevant and effective, providing a secure foundation on your path to financial freedom.

To establish a budget that resonates with minimalist principles, start by examining your expenses. Break them down into categories that make sense for your life. It could be as straightforward as needs, wants, and savings. Be honest with yourself about what truly adds value. Sometimes, this means cutting out expenses that no longer serve your purpose and redirecting funds toward more meaningful endeavors. This isn't about deprivation; it's about intentionality.

Maintaining this financial discipline can indeed be challenging, but it's worth the effort. Regularly review and adjust your budget—it's a reflection of a living, breathing aspect of your life. Periodic check-ins are essential, allowing you to adapt to changes in your circumstances while ensuring your financial goals are still on track. Celebrate the small victories along the way; each step you take strengthens the foundation of your budget.

Think of establishing your budget as planting seeds for future growth. The effort you invest today will nurture your financial garden, allowing it to flourish over time. This approach requires patience, but the rewards—a life aligned with your values and financial peace of mind—make the journey worthwhile. By embracing a budget that works, you move closer to realizing the minimalist, intentional life you aspire to lead.

Creating a Minimalist Budget

A minimalist budget is not just a spreadsheet filled with numbers. It's a reflection of your values and intentions. It's about making room for what truly matters by paring down to essentials and eliminating distractions. Imagine shedding the conventional complexities of budgeting and embracing a streamlined, transparent approach. This section guides you through creating a minimalist budget that supports a balanced and fulfilling life.

Start by examining your current financial situation. Take a candid look at where your money flows each month. Identify categories where your spending aligns with your life goals and those where it doesn't. A minimalist budget is built on the foundation of awareness. Knowing your reality is the first step in shaping a future that resonates with your aspirations.

Once you've assessed your spending, it's time to categorize expenses. Keep your categories simple and mobile. Think "needs," "wants," and "savings." Needs cover essentials like housing, utilities, food, and transportation. Wants may include dining out, entertainment, and leisure activities. Savings should be a priority, not an afterthought. Break these broad categories down into what makes sense for your lifestyle, but resist the urge to over-categorize.

The beauty of a minimalist budget lies in its flexibility. It's not about rigidly sticking to a plan but about aligning your expenditures with your ever-evolving priorities. Begin with the non-negotiables among your needs. Analyze which of these truly reflect your current needs and comfort level, rather than societal expectations or past habits. Your minimalist budget will adapt alongside your personal growth and changing circumstances.

Running a lean budget requires acknowledging wants but not letting them drive you. Intentionality is key. Before making a purchase, pause to ask whether it aligns with your goals or values. By doing this, you instill a habit of conscious consumption, prioritizing experiences and outcomes over mere ownership. It's about an emotional audit as much as a financial one.

In any budgeting approach, the line item for savings deserves careful attention. In a minimalist budget, this takes on a different hue. Here, savings aren't just residual money left over each month but an integral part of your lifestyle. Savings are an enabler of freedom and opportunities, letting you react to challenges and seize possibilities with confidence.

While trimming the fat from your budget, find harmony between austerity and indulgence. Life's joys can't always be swapped for a target in a spreadsheet. A minimalist budget can't work if it feels like punishment, so allow room for small luxuries that bring genuine happiness. Maybe it's a monthly dinner out or a quarterly subscription box; balance your spending with a conscious choice to enhance your life within reason.

Income fluctuation is another reality to consider in your minimalist budget. The secret to handling such ebbs and flows lies in adaptability. Building a buffer within your budget can dampen the impact of unexpected expenses or income dips. This safety net nurtures resilience, allowing you to focus on long-term financial wellness rather than short-term stress.

Monitoring and assessing is an ongoing challenge. Factor in regular evaluations of your budget. Monthly check-ins keep you conscious of your progress and any necessary adjustments. Use this checkpoint as an opportunity to celebrate victories, however small, and to recalibrate goals that may no longer fulfill their original intent.

Think of your minimalist budget as a live document. Don't feel limited to traditional tools, either. Whether you're an app aficionado or prefer pen and paper, choose what keeps you engaged and committed. Consistency over complexity fosters a harmonious dance between numbers, needs, and the narratives of your life.

The ultimate purpose of a minimalist budget is greater than just financial security. It's about creating a rhythmic harmony between money and meaning. It's about freeing up space in your finance plan and, as a result, your life, so you can breathe, dream, and thrive with intention. Let your journey toward a minimalist budget be a path of discovery and empowerment, unlocking a life filled with purpose and grace.

Maintaining Financial Discipline

Maintaining financial discipline is both an art and a science. It's about creating a sustainable lifestyle that aligns with your goals while staying true to a budget that not only works but thrives. This isn't about denying yourself life's pleasures but embracing a mindset that sees beyond immediate gratification. Financial discipline involves a series of decisions, each small yet significant, that steer you toward long-term prosperity. By cultivating habits that reinforce financial discipline, you're laying the groundwork for a future defined by intentional living and financial freedom.

Picture your financial life as a garden. It requires consistent care, attention, and yes, a bit of weeding from time to time. Much like gardening, maintaining financial discipline is about nurturing the right elements and keeping out anything that threatens to entangle your resources. Unlike an overgrown patch of weeds, a well-maintained financial plan thrives with order and purpose. It's about finding that balance where your financial plants grow strong, and your weeds—those frivolous expenses—are kept at bay.

The cornerstone of maintaining financial discipline lies in the daily choices and routines you establish. Start by setting realistic expectations for yourself. Lofty goals may seem inspiring at the onset, but if they're unattainable, they become disheartening barriers rather than motivational benchmarks. Determine your financial limits and capabilities, and work within them. You'll find that progress, however small, tends to snowball into substantial change over time.

Resilience plays a vital role in financial discipline. It's easy to become disheartened when facing setbacks or unforeseen expenses. Yet, resilience transforms these challenges into opportunities for growth. Learn to adapt and reconfigure your plans with each new circumstance. Flexibility doesn't mean straying from your path; it's about evolving with the journey, ensuring that your financial discipline remains intact no matter what life throws your way.

It's essential to monitor your progress regularly. Just as you wouldn't expect a plant to flourish without checking on its growth, your budget needs consistent review. Set aside time each week or month to assess your financial position. Are you staying within your budget? If not, what adjustments need to be made? This practice not only keeps you accountable but also provides insight into spending patterns and areas where discipline might be faltering. The more attuned you become to these nuances, the easier it is to make informed decisions moving forward.

One practical approach to maintaining discipline is through automation. By setting up automatic transfers to savings accounts or investments, you're prioritizing savings without relying solely on willpower. This "set it and forget it" strategy can help you stay on track even during busier periods when financial management might not be at the forefront of your mind. With certain elements of your budget on autopilot, your energy can focus on fine-tuning other areas.

Engage in self-reflection regularly. Financial discipline isn't just about external actions but internal alignment as well. Reflect on your financial habits and consider whether they still serve your long-term objectives. Are there areas where you've become complacent? Use these moments of introspection to recommit to your goals and reinforce new, improved habits that align with your minimalist lifestyle.

Crafting a lifestyle that's both fulfilling and frugal demands creativity. Find joy in experiences that don't break the bank. Embrace hobbies and activities that enrich your life without draining your wallet, whether it's a homemade meal with friends, a hike in nature, or exploring urban museums on free admission days. By seeking fulfillment in simple pleasures, you reinforce a disciplined approach to spending and expand your repertoire of enjoyable, low-cost experiences.

A supportive community can further bolster your financial discipline. Surround yourself with like-minded individuals who share your financial philosophies and values. Engage in discussions about savings strategies, budget-friendly tips, or accountability partnerships. These connections not only provide practical advice but also offer encouragement and validation when the road to financial discipline feels daunting.

Finally, remember that financial discipline is a journey, not a destination. Celebrate the milestones you achieve along the way, no matter how minor they may seem. Each one is a testament to your perseverance and commitment to a minimalist financial lifestyle. By acknowledging these successes, you're more likely to retain your motivation and sustain your financial discipline over the long haul.

Chapter 7: Reducing Debt

Debt, for many, is like a shadow that looms over every financial decision, limiting freedom and adding stress to our lives. In the journey toward financial liberation, reducing debt stands as a pivotal milestone. It's not an easy path, but with intentional actions and a strategic mindset, it can be navigated successfully. Before we jump into the strategies, it's essential to acknowledge the emotional strain that debt can have on individuals and families. Debt isn't just numbers on a page; it's often tied to deeper feelings of regret, anxiety, and overwhelm.

Approaching the task of reducing debt requires a blend of courage, commitment, and compassion towards oneself. Start with creating a clear picture of what you owe—lay it all out. List each debt, the interest rate, minimum payments, and the total amount owed. Understanding the whole landscape is the first empowering step, providing a sense of control over what might have felt chaotic.

Next, let's consider the strategies that work effectively for eliminating debt. Two popular methods come to mind—the avalanche and snowball techniques. The avalanche method involves paying off debts in order from the highest to the lowest interest rate, which saves you money on interest in the long run. Alternatively, the snowball method focuses on paying off the smallest debts first, offering psychological wins as each balance is cleared. Choose the method that aligns with your financial goals and personal motivation. Remember, different strategies work for different minds.

An accountability system is invaluable here. Whether it's sharing your journey with a trusted friend or using an app to track repayments, accountability can increase your chances of sticking to the plan. Celebrate each victory, no matter the size because every step forward is a step closer to freedom.

Reducing debt also calls for a critical look at your spending habits. Simplifying life doesn't just mean purging physical possessions; it's about eliminating unnecessary financial burdens too. Ask yourself what purchases truly add value to your life and which ones are merely distractions. Redirect funds from non-essential expenses towards debt reduction. This isn't about deprivation; it's about crafting a lifestyle that's more aligned with your values and goals.

Along the way, it's vital to remain flexible. Life is unpredictable, and sometimes unexpected costs arise. Prepare for these by setting aside a small emergency fund, something modest but enough to handle life's hiccups without derailing your debt reduction progress. This buffer acts as a safety net, keeping you on your path amid the waves of uncertainty.

Ultimately, reducing debt isn't merely an exercise in financial strategy; it's a profound act of self-care. As debts disappear, so too does the weight they carry. Financial space is created not just in your accounts but also in your mind, allowing room for joy, creativity, and other pursuits that may have been previously stifled. Cherish the journey, and know that every challenging moment brings you closer to a future unencumbered by debt.

Strategies for Rapid Debt Elimination

Rapid debt elimination is a cornerstone of achieving financial freedom. It's about shaking off the shackles of debt and transforming your financial landscape with determination and clarity. For those seeking simplified and intentional living, expunging debt efficiently aligns with living minimally and focusing on what truly matters. Shuffling through layers of financial obligations without a clear strategy can be daunting, but you're not alone in this journey. With the right strategies, you can turn what feels like an endless uphill climb into a manageable path with progress at every step.

First, let's talk about the power of mindset, the heart of any rapid debt elimination strategy. You need to make debt reduction a priority, focusing your thoughts and energy on clearing financial burdens. The process begins with a solid commitment, one where you're fully invested in seeing through. Envisioning a debt-free life helps keep this motivation alive. Imagine the peace that comes with no longer being tethered to creditors, where your resources are your own, and every dollar isn't spoken for before it hits your checking account.

To take on this challenge, start by creating a comprehensive list of all your debts. Include every detail: the type of debt, outstanding balances, interest rates, and minimum payments. This list is your map and baseline. Making your debts visible makes them real; it's a crucial step in taking control. Next, prioritize these debts. Two popular methods—debt snowball and debt avalanche—can be tailored to fit your needs.

The debt snowball method involves tackling your smallest debts first, working your way up to larger ones. This approach gives quick wins and boosts motivation since knocking out smaller debts can build momentum. There's something incredibly satisfying about removing names from the list and seeing it become shorter. Conversely, the debt avalanche strategy targets debts with the highest interest rates first, saving you money on interest over time and reducing the overall cost of your debt. Analyze your financial situation to determine which method speaks to you; the key is to start and stay consistent.

After choosing your preferred method, it's time to develop a realistic and effective budget plan. An enabling budget is crucial for successful debt elimination. Aim to allocate any surplus funds toward your debt, but remember, the journey to financial freedom isn't about deprivation. It's about making intentional choices. Limit unnecessary spending and redirect those funds toward your debt repayment plans. Celebrate small wins when you knock down those balances. Rewards don't have to be financial—they could mean time spent on a favorite hobby or simply enjoying a moment of peace knowing you're moving in the right direction.

To accelerate your progress, look for ways to increase your income. Could you freelance a skill, take on temporary part-time work, or perhaps sell unwanted items? Even small amounts added to monthly payments significantly decrease overall debt in the long run. Side hustles offer not just monetary benefits but also a sense of agency, tangibly impacting your debt repayment journey.

Automating your payments ensures you won't miss a due date, avoiding late fees that can set back the clock on your progress. Set up automatic transfers for debts with the most urgent balances or higher interest rates. Automation helps make debt repayment routine, like any other bill, relegating it to something that no longer consumes mental energy.

While addressing the present, don't shy away from keeping an eye on the future impacts of your debt repayment strategies. Construct a contingency plan for unexpected expenses like medical bills or car repairs. Building an emergency fund alongside paying down debt might seem counterintuitive, but it's essential to prevent going deeper into debt when life throws inevitable surprises.

Consider consolidating your debts if it reduces your total monthly payments or interest rates. Personal loans often have lower interest than credit cards and can simplify multiple monthly payments into one—often at a fixed rate. This step should be approached with caution, ensuring that it aligns with your long-term financial goals and does not exacerbate the problem.

Remember, the journey to erase debt isn't just about money; it's a lifestyle adjustment. Minimalist living goes hand in hand with feeling financial freedom. Embed the principles of intentionality and mindfulness into your spending habits. Question each purchase's necessity, and value needs over wants. Let this practice extend beyond a debt-free life to guide future financial decisions.

Your emotional wellbeing plays as crucial a role in debt elimination as your financial strategies. Creditors can be persistent, and stress is a given when managing debt. Find support through family, friends, or financial advisors who are willing to listen and offer advice. Getting through tough times is easier with a cheering squad and expert guidance.

In this quest for rapid debt elimination, tether your identity not to the numbers or balances but to your unwavering commitment to freedom. Reflect on progress regularly, remain adaptable to new tactics, and continue learning. Assess your plans, re-evaluate priorities, and be open to adjusting as life and finances change. Rapid debt elimination requires tenacity and vision, key elements that leave you ready to embrace the full potential of financial independence and simplified living. Imagine not only a future without debt but a world where you direct your financial story with clarity and confidence.

Navigating the Path to Financial Freedom

Transitioning from the heavy burden of debt to a place of financial freedom can feel like an overwhelming journey, but it's crucial to remember that each small step accumulates into significant progress. This chapter, focused on reducing debt, isn't merely about numbers and payments—it's about forging a path toward a more liberated and intentional life. Imagine debt as a dense forest fog, and every thoughtful action you take serves to disperse it, illuminating the way forward. Many people have traveled this path successfully, and their experiences provide a roadmap full of practical guidance and the assurance that financial freedom is achievable.

First, acknowledge the emotions tied to debt. It can evoke feelings of guilt, stress, and even shame. But these feelings need not define your relationship with money anymore. Understanding that debt is a common part of many financial journeys helps strip away some of the isolation that can accompany it. You're not alone, and the load you're carrying can be lightened by embracing new, more productive financial practices. The goal upfront is to foster a healthier mindset, one that views debt not as an insurmountable barrier, but as a challenge that you're entirely capable of overcoming.

One of the most powerful tools in debt reduction is the practice of prioritization. Start by listing your debts, not to overwhelm yourself, but to clearly see what's there. While facing this list might feel intimidating, it is the first step in reclaiming control. Once you have your list, decide which debts to tackle first. Many find success with the "snowball" method, where they pay off the smallest debts first for quick wins and psychological momentum. Others opt for the "avalanche" approach, first eliminating debts with the highest interest rates, which over time may save more money. Choose the strategy that resonates most with your current situation and mindset.

Budgeting is an essential companion on the journey to financial freedom. A well-curated budget is like a compass that keeps you oriented and on course. Design your budget around your financial reality, incorporating both necessary expenses and modest allowances for life's pleasures to prevent burnout. Discipline is nurtured over time, so don't be discouraged by initial missteps. Regularly revisiting and adjusting your budget enables it to evolve with your needs, ensuring it remains a reliable guide throughout your journey.

Additionally, think of income not just in terms of your current paycheck but as opportunities to expand your financial horizon. Exploring side hustles or freelance opportunities can provide extra funds dedicated solely to debt repayment. These ventures need not be permanent but can make a substantial impact when applied with purpose and clarity. Consider skills you already possess that could be monetized with minimal upfront investment—writing, consulting, or crafting, for instance. This increase in cash flow helps chip away at debt more rapidly, accelerating your path to freedom.

Resilience often comes from community and support. Engage with those who have faced similar challenges, whether through local groups, online forums, or even supportive friends and family members. These connections offer encouragement and hold you accountable, reducing the mental load that debt can place on an individual. They can also be a rich source of tips and financial strategies you might not have considered.

Recognize the importance of celebrating milestones along the way. Each cleared debt or successful month within your budget contributes to the larger goal, and acknowledging these achievements reinforces your commitment and endurance. These celebrations need not be extravagant or costly; they can be simple acts of self-appreciation that affirm the progress made. Taking time to affirm your progress enhances motivation and ensures that the process is not just a sprint to the next payment but a transformative journey toward a lasting, debt-free future.

In parallel, it's beneficial to cultivate a vision of what financial freedom looks like for you. Is it as simple as not worrying about monthly bills or as expansive as planning future investments or philanthropic endeavors? Holding onto this vision provides clarity and motivation, transforming what may feel like hardship into hope and purpose. Imagining a life unhindered by financial constraints invites a sense of liberation, which can illuminate your daily financial decisions, making sacrifices feel less like deprivation and more like strategic choices for a better future.

The significance of a tailored financial education can't be underestimated. Understanding personal finance concepts, even at a foundational level, can alter how you view money management, saving, and investing. Whether through books, courses, or mentorship, this knowledge empowers you to take informed actions that are aligned with both your current and future goals, transitioning you from mere debt management to true wealth building. Consider these learnings as investments in yourself, vital in constructing a more secure financial foundation to sustain you long after the debts have vanished.

Finally, remember that the ultimate goal is not just to eliminate debt but to build a robust framework for ongoing financial independence. This means integrating all you've learned into a comprehensive plan that includes budgeting, saving, investing, and continuous learning. By aligning your financial behaviors with this broader aspiration, each debt payment takes you closer to not only a balance of zero but to a life rich with possibilities and free from financial constraints.

The path to financial freedom, while challenging, is not insurmountable. By embracing your financial reality, taking intentional actions, and constantly nurturing your future vision, you'll find that the journey itself becomes as enriching as the destination. Financial freedom isn't a myth; it's a series of deliberate choices that, when made consistently, lead you to the liberation and peace you seek. The keys are patience, perseverance, and a steadfast belief in your ability to transform your financial life for the better.

Chapter 8: Saving with Purpose

The pathway to financial freedom often demands more than just consistent effort—it calls for intention, clarity, and thoughtfulness. In this chapter, we delve into the essence of saving with purpose. It's more than watching pennies; it's about aligning your savings habits with your broader life values. By doing so, your savings strategy not only supports your financial goals but also enriches your life's journey.

Think about saving as cultivating a garden. At first, you prepare the soil, tending to it with care and attention. You plant seeds that you know will take time to grow into something meaningful. Similarly, when we save with purpose, we're planting seeds for our future. We're intentional about the spaces we nourish and the resources we allocate.

Your savings strategy should reflect your life's unique narrative. Recognize what matters most to you and allow those priorities to guide your financial decisions. Work backward from your dreams and values, understanding that each dollar saved is a building block toward the life you envision. This process transforms saving from a mere task into a deliberate practice with clear objectives.

Simplifying savings strategies might mean shedding some preconceived notions. Instead of relying on complicated investment schemes or aggressive saving tactics that strain your daily life, anchor yourself in minimalist principles. Focus on what genuinely contributes to your long-term vision, and let simplicity drive your approach. This might involve automating savings to eliminate decision fatigue or adopting a 'pay yourself first' mindset.

Long-term success in savings often hinges on prioritization. Where we place our priorities determines how effectively we meet our financial milestones. It's essential to have a clear sense of hierarchy. Create a savings plan that respects both immediate needs and future aspirations, balancing short-term sacrifices with long-term rewards. *Consider the role of an emergency fund*, ensuring it gets the attention it deserves while also prioritizing goals like retirement or homeownership. These aren't just targets but steps toward a fulfilling life.

What emerges from saving with purpose is a profound sense of empowerment. It's not merely about accumulating wealth—it's about crafting a financial life that mirrors your values and supports your ambitions. When your saving decisions align with your purpose, they become less of a burden and more of a joyful commitment to yourself and your future.

Finally, keep the end goals flexible. As life evolves, so too should your savings strategy. Embrace the changes; don't fear adjusting your plans to accommodate new priorities or life stages. Regularly review and realign your goals to ensure they truly reflect who you are and where you want to be. In doing so, your savings remain a living narrative, continuously adapting and growing just as you do.

Embracing a Simplistic Savings Strategy

Saving doesn't have to be complicated. When you let go of unnecessary complexities and focus on what truly matters, saving becomes a more manageable and rewarding process. Effective saving doesn't rely on fancy software, nor does it necessitate intricate spreadsheets adorned with pie charts. Instead, it's about intentionally channeling your resources toward your goals, combining simplicity with purpose.

Imagine your savings journey as a gentle river course. With a clear purpose, free from obstructions, its flow is smooth and constant. Just as a river is fed by consistent streams of water, your savings strategy thrives on regular, intentional contributions. It's not always about putting down vast sums; rather, it's the habitual act of saving that builds a robust financial future.

One of the initial steps is gaining clarity on what simplicity in savings looks like for you. This clarity starts with understanding your financial priorities. Ask yourself, "What do I need to secure a life of ease and fulfillment?" The answer will guide you in setting aside what might clutter your financial environment. Prioritizing saving doesn't mean sacrificing all pleasures; instead, it means making choices that align with your bigger picture.

Minimalism plays a pivotal role here. It's about adopting a mindset where less is truly more. With minimalism, savings strategies don't compete for your attention with the allure of unnecessary expenditures. Instead, your focus remains on steady, purposeful growth over time. This shift begins by embracing the idea that every dollar saved is a conscious decision to invest in your future well-being.

Now, let's touch on the tools – or lack thereof. While high-tech financial tools abound, a simple approach recommends traditional methods, such as straightforward budgeting or merely setting aside a daily amount. The key isn't in the tool itself, but in the discipline and habit it fosters. This doesn't mean abandoning all forms of technology; rather, use them sparingly and purposefully, ensuring they add value and clarity to your saving goals.

Consistent Methods Matter

The consistency of your approach is far more important than the complexity of your methods. Setting up automatic transfers from checking to savings ensures you're contributing without even thinking about it. This kind of automation can minimize decision fatigue, allowing you to save with ease and regularity. It's about creating a financial environment where saving happens naturally, with minimal interference from daily fluctuations in your mood or circumstances.

Additionally, one effective strategy is to reframe your perspective on spending versus saving. Whenever faced with a financial decision, ask: "How does this align with my values, and does it support my path to financial freedom?" This mindset, deeply rooted in minimalism, ensures that every choice either nurtures your resources or redirects them toward what matters most.

A simplified savings strategy also encourages reassessing wants and needs. The stark clarity of understanding the difference can be liberating and financially rewarding. Needs are essential for survival and comfort, while wants are desires that, while pleasing, may not provide long-term satisfaction. By prioritizing needs, you naturally funnel resources toward saving goals that support your overall financial health.

The concept of "paying yourself first" is quintessentially minimalist and an excellent practice within a simplistic savings strategy. Before bills, before leisure, set aside a portion of your income. This ensures that the future you envision has the necessary resources you're diligently working to accumulate.

Nurturing Simplicity as a Lifestyle
As you embrace this strategy, nurturing simplicity doesn't just stay confined to your finances. It begins to influence every part of your life. From decluttering your physical space to decluttering your mind, the habits formed while simplifying your savings often spill over into other areas. This naturally promotes a harmonious balance, where your financial life aligns seamlessly with your intentional living goals.

Yet, life is anything but predictable. Unexpected expenses do arise, but this does not mean straying from simplicity. Instead, these moments are opportunities to test and refine your strategy. Perhaps it's about drawing from an emergency fund that's been part of your saving plan all along, or reconsidering some expenses momentarily to stay on track with your goals. The beauty of a simplistic strategy is its flexibility, and this adaptability assures that when life's wind shifts, you're ready to adjust your sails toward the direction of growth.

When enthusiasm wanes, tapping into your underlying motivations is essential. Remember why you started, envision the life you aim to sculpt, and focus on the peace and security your savings efforts bring. Financial freedom isn't a far-off destination; it's the everyday joy and confidence that comes from knowing you're on the path with purpose.

Ultimately, embracing a simplistic savings strategy isn't about deprivation or strict austerity. It's about curating your financial landscape in a way that resonates with simplicity and intentionality. So, celebrate the small victories along the way. Each step forward, however tiny, is significant, for it not only inches you closer to financial security but also echoes the mindful and purposeful existence you strive for.

Prioritizing Savings for Long-term Success

Saving money isn't just about putting aside what's left after expenses; it's about making it a central part of our financial lives. It's about intentionality and understanding that each dollar saved brings us a step closer to our long-term goals. Building a robust savings philosophy involves a mindset shift that transforms saving from an afterthought to a priority.

Imagine your savings not as deprivation, but as empowerment. It's the choice to prioritize future comfort over fleeting indulgences. By adopting this perspective, every small sacrifice today becomes a gift to your future self. Embracing this outlook can be incredibly rewarding, as it aligns your daily financial decisions with your long-term aspirations.

One effective strategy is to automate your savings. By setting up automatic transfers from your checking account to a savings account as soon as you get paid, saving becomes seamless and almost effortless. This system removes the temptation to spend what you might otherwise allocate haphazardly. Over time, watching your savings grow becomes a source of motivation, reinforcing a positive cycle of saving and investing in your future.

Creating specific savings goals can provide the clarity and direction needed to keep your financial journey on track. Whether it's an emergency fund, a down payment for a home, or a travel fund, having a definitive goal makes saving purposeful. These goals act as beacons, illuminating the path ahead and providing the determination needed to navigate financial challenges. Ask yourself what truly matters, what destinations you wish to reach, and let these answers guide your savings ambitions.

However, even the best-laid plans require periodic reviews. It's essential to evaluate your savings strategy regularly, ensuring it aligns with your evolving life circumstances and aspirations. This constant reassessment prevents stagnation and keeps you attuned to new opportunities or adjustments that might need to be made. A flexible approach to your savings plan preserves its relevance and effectiveness over time.

We all know life's unpredictable, which is why establishing an emergency fund is paramount. Consider it a financial cushion or safety net, should unexpected expenses arise. Typically, a fund covering three to six months' worth of living expenses is recommended, but the right amount varies depending on personal circumstances and risk tolerance. This fund can offer a comfort that allows you to pursue other financial goals with confidence, knowing you have a fallback plan.

Harnessing the power of compound interest elevates your savings strategy from simply accumulating funds to generating wealth. Starting early in life is particularly advantageous, though it's never too late to benefit from this powerful financial tool. By saving consistently over the years, even modest contributions can grow significantly, thanks to the compounding effect. It's a simple principle but profoundly effective in building wealth over the long term.

Furthermore, aligning your savings with your values adds a layer of fulfillment to financial planning. Are you saving to support a future lifestyle that reflects your passions, or to contribute to causes you care about? By ensuring that your savings goals match your personal values, you create a holistic approach to wealth-building that supports both financial health and personal wellbeing. This alignment turns saving into a meaningful practice rather than a mere financial chore.

While it's crucial to focus on long-term goals, it's also important to strike a balance that allows for moments of enjoyment along the way. Here's where the art of moderation comes into play. By planning for small, guilt-free splurges among your larger savings goals, you'll maintain a healthy relationship with your finances. The key is to relish these moments without compromising your commitment to your future.

It's easy to get off track with countless temptations offering instant gratification. But perseverance in saving requires both discipline and, occasionally, the wisdom to indulge within reason. Balancing impulse and intentionality ensures that your savings habits are sustainable, creating a lifestyle that supports both present satisfaction and future security. Remember, the journey to financial freedom through simplified and intentional living is a deeply personal one. Each step in prioritizing savings for long-term success requires a commitment to understanding oneself and one's goals. This consciousness transforms saving from a passive accumulation of funds into an active participant in your life's dreams and aspirations. In doing so, financial freedom becomes not just an endpoint, but a lived experience throughout the journey.

Chapter 9: Investing the Minimalist Way

In a world that often encourages excess, minimalist investing beckons us toward simplicity and intentionality. It invites us to strip away the noise and complexity that typically shroud the investment landscape, focusing instead on what truly matters: thoughtful allocation, patience, and clarity. There's a serene elegance to a minimalist investment portfolio, one that mirrors the principles of minimalist living by focusing on what's essential, avoiding overindulgence, and seeking long-term growth.

Minimalist investing isn't about buying every hot stock or jumping on the latest market trend. It's about crafting a strategy that aligns with your goals, values, and risk tolerance. Picture it as cultivating a garden. You don't plant every seed you come across; you choose what to sow based on your needs and the environment you're in. A minimalist portfolio reflects this mindset, emphasizing quality over quantity. Rather than chasing every investment opportunity, focus on a handful of stable, historically sound choices that align with your long-term vision.

Consider diversification, a cornerstone of risk management. While traditional views might push for spreading investments across a wide array of financial instruments, minimalist investing suggests a more considered approach. Diversification should not mean complexity for complexity's sake. It's about balancing your portfolio to manage risk without overwhelming yourself with unwieldy intricacies. Think of it like curating an art collection — every piece should have a place and purpose, contributing to the harmony and balance of the whole.

For those influenced by technology, investing has become more accessible and transparent than ever. Minimalists can leverage this digital era by utilizing low-cost index funds and exchange-traded funds (ETFs), which reflect the market's overall performance without requiring daily management. These instruments embody the minimalist ethos: simplicity, reliability, and efficiency. They offer a practical way to grow wealth steadily, all while reducing the stress and decision fatigue that can come with trying to outsmart the market.

Yet, even in low-cost investments, patience is paramount. The essence of investing the minimalist way is cultivating a mindset that foresees and withstands market fluctuations. This requires a certain grace and presence of mind, understanding that time in the market often beats timing the market. By engaging with your investments with mindfulness, you learn to weather the inevitable storms, confident in the knowledge that your careful preparation lays a solid foundation for growth.

At its core, minimalist investing encourages us to realign our financial decisions with our life's greater purpose. It's a reflection of our values, ensuring that our investments enhance, rather than overshadow, our pursuit of a meaningful life. This chapter, then, becomes more than a guide; it is an invitation. It calls on you to ponder deeply about each financial choice, to let go of the complexities that do not serve you, and to embrace a peaceful, productive balance in your wealth-building journey.

Ultimately, the minimalist way of investing is not merely a strategy but a philosophy, urging you to simplify, to be deliberate, and to focus on the beautiful synergy between financial growth and intentional living.

Investment Strategies for Simple Living

To embrace simplicity in investing often means cutting through the noise and focusing on what truly matters. It's about realizing that complexity doesn't necessarily equal better returns. When you choose investment strategies that align with a minimalist lifestyle, you're not just streamlining your financial portfolio; you're aligning your investments with your values. This intersection of finance and personal philosophy is where minimalism can have a powerful, transformational effect.

Let's start with an understanding that investing as a minimalist isn't about abstaining from the markets. Instead, it's about making careful choices that reflect your priorities. You don't need endless trades; what you need is clarity and purpose. Seek out investments that resonate with your life goals, and remember, a minimalist doesn't look for excess; they look for value.

Minimalist investing urges us to shun the clutter of overly diversified portfolios which aim for every trendy asset class. Instead, focus on deliberate diversification, creating a portfolio that is resilient but not overburdened. The key here is to ensure that every investment serves a meaningful purpose in your long-term plan.

Hand in hand with this, simple living aligns well with long-term investing. It's a strategy that discourages frantic responses to the whims of the market. Instead, patience becomes a virtue, allowing compound growth to work its magic. Decades-old wisdom teaches us the power of compound interest, yet it's a concept that thrives in an environment of steady calm — a hallmark of the minimalist investor.

For those living simply, index funds are often the cornerstone of a streamlined investment strategy. These funds, which mirror the performance of a broad market index, offer a balance of risk and reward with minimal maintenance required. They embody the minimalist ideal by freeing you from the constant need to tweak your portfolio based on market trends. What could be simpler than letting your money grow quietly in the backdrop of your life?

Another principle of minimalist investing is the idea of authenticity; investing in what you genuinely understand and care about. It's not about joining the bandwagon; it's about making thoughtful decisions that reflect who you are and what you believe in. Passion and knowledge provide the confidence needed to invest in a way that's intentional and true to your values.

Moreover, there's unique satisfaction in considering ethical and sustainable investments. These choices often align inherently with a lifestyle that values simplicity and sustainability. They challenge us to think about the broader impact of our investing decisions, intertwining personal gain with positive societal and environmental outcomes. Thus, minimalism is not just a personal journey but a potential catalyst for broader change.

Managing investment risk is another critical aspect of investing the minimalist way. Instead of engaging in high-risk ventures or speculative investments, minimalists often lean toward a strategy that's safe yet considerate of their need for growth. Balancing safety nets like bonds with growth engines like equities is crucial for a diversified and robust portfolio.

Consider the role of cash management in this minimalist approach. While it's important not to let cash holdings overtake growth assets in your portfolio, having some liquidity offers peace of mind during unpredictable financial periods. Cash isn't just a hedge against volatility; it's freedom, ready to be mobilized for new opportunities or unforeseen challenges.

Importantly, the minimalist investor is disciplined, not just financially but mentally. The endless cycle of economic news, predictions, and analyses can lead to anxiety and impulsive decisions, eroding prudent investment practices. Minimalism teaches the wisdom of tuning out the unnecessary clamor, focusing instead on enduring principles and proven strategies.

Lastly, while the journey of investing can be deeply personal, remember that you don't have to walk it alone. Lean into community and relationships with like-minded individuals. This collaborative spirit can provide fresh insights and mutual support, crucial for maintaining minimalist practices in investing.

In intertwining simple living with your investment strategy, you create more than just wealth. You build a life that aligns with your highest values, offering both financial freedom and the joy of simplicity. It's less about numbers on a screen and more about crafting a meaningful legacy that reflects who you truly are.

Diversification and Risk Management
Investing in a minimalist way often feels like a dance between simple living and the inherent complexities of financial markets. We seek tranquility and clarity, yet the world of investing tends to be chaotic and unpredictable. However, navigating this landscape doesn't have to disrupt our pursuit of a minimalist lifestyle. At the heart of this balance lies the concept of diversification and risk management. It's about spreading your investments wisely to reduce potential pitfalls and ensuring that your financial journey remains as seamless and stress-free as possible.

Diversification acts as the guiding principle for reducing risk without overwhelming complexity. Imagine your investments as a hearty stew, with each ingredient playing a crucial role in balance and flavor. By spreading your investments across various asset classes, you're not putting all your financial eggs in one basket. Whether it's stocks, bonds, real estate, or even ventures like peer-to-peer lending, each has a part to play. This strategy allows you to absorb shocks in one area without devastating your entire portfolio.

The essence of risk management begins with understanding your own risk tolerance. It's an intimate reflection of your financial personality and goals. Some of us prefer the adrenaline rush of high-stakes investing, while others value the calm of stable, slower growth. Recognizing where you stand is the first step. This understanding guides the choice of diversification strategies that align with your values and comfort levels.

Minimalist investing doesn't require expert-level knowledge or advanced strategies. In fact, simplicity often yields the best results. Index funds are a classic example of this minimalist approach. They allow you to own a slice of the market without needing to pick and choose individual winners and losers. With lower fees and a long track record of steady growth, index funds align perfectly with a minimalist philosophy—efficiency without excess.

Risk management doesn't mean eliminating uncertainty; rather, it's about mitigating its impact. Setting clear boundaries with asset allocation is one such technique. If preserving wealth takes precedence, allocating more towards bonds might be wise. For those with higher growth targets and longer timelines, stocks may dominate. Regular rebalancing of your portfolio ensures that your asset distribution remains aligned with your initial risk profile, adding another layer of stability.

It's crucial to remember that diversification doesn't guarantee a profit or protect against a loss. Instead, it serves as a buffer. In times of market volatility, a diversified portfolio can help smooth out returns and reduce the whiplash of market swings. Just as a diverse garden can weather storms better than a monoculture, your diversified portfolio stands resilient through economic ebbs and flows.

An often-overlooked aspect of risk management is emotional discipline. Staying the course, especially when markets are jittery, can be daunting. However, sticking with your plans and not making impulsive decisions based on fear or hype can bode well for your financial health. Reacting to market noise by making sudden shifts can undo the benefits of careful diversification.

Consider, too, the significance of regularly reviewing your investment strategy. As life progresses, so do your financial goals and risk tolerance. Periodic assessments ensure that your diversified portfolio continues to reflect your evolving needs and minimalist principles. Such adjustments may be subtle tweaks or comprehensive overhauls, but they are vital in maintaining harmony between your investments and life values.

Incorporating risk management into your financial routine doesn't require vast resources or complex computations. Visualize it as a series of thoughtful practices reinforcing each other—a well-balanced meal rather than an extravagant buffet. Such mindfulness aligns with the minimalist ethos, promoting a sense of financial security without the need to sacrifice peace of mind.

Ultimately, embracing diversification and risk management within the minimalist framework empowers you to cultivate wealth with intention and purpose. It's about creating a financial life that's not only robust and resilient but also aligns with your overarching values. By keeping things simple and honest, you're designing an investment strategy that perfectly complements the minimalist lifestyle—a journey towards financial freedom that's as thoughtful as it is fulfilling.

Chapter 10: Building Passive Income

Building passive income is a journey, not a destination. It's the art of making money while you sleep, freeing you from the relentless cycle of trading time for money. Embracing passive income means embracing freedom—the freedom to choose how you spend your days, the freedom to pursue passions that excite you, and the freedom to design a life that doesn't compromise your values. But how do you get started on this journey? Let's explore some pathways to build streams of income that work even when you're not.

Passive income isn't about overnight success or quick wins but about setting up smart, simple systems that sustain themselves with minimal effort from you. Think about it like planting a garden. It takes planning, patience, and a bit of nurturing at the start. Once established, though, your garden can flourish with less intensive care, yielding rewards season after season. Identifying the right passive income opportunities that align with your minimalist values and lifestyle is crucial. Often the simplest approaches turn out to be the most effective.

An excellent starting point is to evaluate assets you already own. Consider renting out a spare room or your car when it's not in use. Platforms like Airbnb or Turo can facilitate this, turning underutilized assets into income generators. These approaches require some upfront effort but once set, they largely run on autopilot. Understanding market demand and pricing can maximize your earnings while staying aligned with your primary lifestyle.

Another path to consider is dividend investing—a way to earn money from the stocks you own without having to sell them. Selecting dividend-paying companies can provide an ongoing income stream. However, it's essential to research and choose companies with strong, stable financial performance and a history of paying dividends regularly. This strategy requires a foundational understanding of the stock market and the patience to weather its fluctuations. Over the long term, reinvesting dividends can significantly compound your wealth.

If you're someone who enjoys creating, consider developing digital products. Writing an e-book, creating an online course, or designing printables taps into your creative potential while setting the stage for passive income. Each of these requires upfront work but, once completed, can be sold repeatedly with minimal additional effort. Focus on creating value—what are people struggling with, and how can your skills or knowledge offer a solution?

A less obvious but equally impactful source of passive income is building a community through content creation. Whether it's a blog, a YouTube channel, or a social media presence, providing consistent value can attract a loyal audience. It opens up revenue channels through advertising, sponsorships, or memberships. While this approach requires persistence and authenticity, the satisfaction of sharing your journey and insights with others can be rewarding far beyond the financial gains.

In pursuing passive income, it's vital to steer clear of methods that overcomplicate your life or necessitate constant intervention. This journey should not conflict with the principles of simplicity and intentionality you've been cultivating. Consider automation tools that help manage these income streams without constant oversight. Balancing systems with simplicity ensures your passive income strategies enhance rather than encumber your life.

Moreover, passive income isn't just about accumulating wealth. It's about aligning your income with a lifestyle that supports your values. As you build these income sources, reassess them periodically. Do they still serve your lifestyle aspirations? Are they compatible with your work-life balance, personal growth, and family commitments?

In the end, the most meaningful wealth isn't measured in dollars or possessions but in time and freedom of choice. Choose projects that resonate with your heart and allow you to express your true self. Let your pursuit of passive income be a reflection of your journey towards a life of purpose, alignment, and joy. Take this chapter as a seed, plant it, tend to it, and watch your passive income grow, empowering you to live life on your terms.

Identifying Passive Income Opportunities

In the journey toward financial freedom, identifying passive income opportunities stands as a pivotal step. It embodies the philosophy of earning without being tethered to a nine-to-five grind. The prospect of generating income while focusing on life's more meaningful pursuits is nothing short of liberating. Yet, finding these opportunities requires an intentional approach, aligning perfectly with a life of simplicity and purpose.

To start, let's explore the core concept of passive income. Passive income is earnings derived from ventures in which a person is not actively involved. While some involvement and maintenance are often required, the primary goal is to create a revenue stream that necessitates minimal day-to-day effort. Understanding this framework helps us seek opportunities that fit our minimalist values, bypassing ventures that demand excessive oversight or a complicated setup.

Real estate investment often springs to mind when discussing passive income, and for good reason. Owning rental properties, for example, can provide a reliable income stream. However, it's crucial to understand the initial time, effort, and resources needed to make such a venture successful. Evaluating the local market, understanding tenant laws, and possibly hiring a property manager are part of this process. While substantial, the rewards of well-chosen real estate investments can significantly bolster your financial independence journey.

If real estate feels too daunting or out of reach, consider the growing sphere of digital assets. Creating and selling digital products—such as e-books, online courses, or printables—can yield passive income with the right strategy. These products offer long-lasting revenue potential since they can be sold repeatedly without the need for significant additional effort. This option aligns with minimalist principles by using existing knowledge and skills to create value.

Similarly, affiliate marketing presents another straightforward path. By sharing products or services through a blog, social media, or a website, individuals earn a commission on sales driven by their referrals. The key here is authenticity, choosing products aligned with your values, and ensuring that your audience genuinely benefits. Investing time in building an online presence and trust can yield dividends without extensive ongoing involvement.

Investing in dividend stocks is another pathway worth delving into. This approach involves purchasing shares of companies that distribute a portion of their earnings as dividends to shareholders. For those inclined toward financial markets, dividend investing can provide a steady income stream. The choice of stocks should, however, align with a minimalist investment strategy, ensuring a diversified portfolio that balances risk with potential reward.

Moreover, peer-to-peer lending platforms have democratized the lending space, offering individuals the chance to earn interest. By lending money to others in need, you can receive interest payments over time. This method requires due diligence to mitigate default risks, but when managed wisely, it can be a gratifying way to put your money to work.

Royalties from creative endeavors, like writing a book or licensing a piece of music, can also form a source of passive income. Although creating such works involves an upfront commitment, the subsequent passive income potential is rewarding. Embracing inherent creativity allows you to produce something of lasting value that continues to generate revenue.

It's worth underscoring the importance of diversifying passive income sources. Just as in investing, relying on a single stream can expose you to unnecessary risk. Diversification ensures that if one income source wanes, others can offset the loss. A varied portfolio of passive income streams offers stability and enhances financial resilience.

As you identify these opportunities, align them with your skills, interests, and current resources. The pursuit of passive income should not breed stress or parallel the fast-paced hustle culture. Instead, it should integrate seamlessly into your lifestyle, offering financial benefits while allowing you to live intentionally.

Remember, the essence of generating passive income lies in the balance—it should complement your life, not complicate it. By approaching these opportunities with mindfulness and strategy, we align our financial paths with our minimalist ethos. In doing so, we're not just building wealth, but we're also crafting a life that resonates with our core values of simplicity and freedom.

As you embark on this journey, stay open to learning and adapting. The landscape of passive income is dynamic, and opportunities evolve with technology and societal changes. Keeping an eye on these shifts, learning from peers, and staying curious will help you in continually refining your passive income approach, ensuring it remains effective and aligned with your lifestyle.

Sustaining Wealth Through Minimal Effort

Imagine a life where wealth flows to you like a gentle stream, requiring little maintenance yet constantly nourishing your financial landscape. This isn't a fantasy—it's a reality you can achieve by building passive income streams thoughtfully and strategically. The key lies in creating a solid foundation that enables your wealth to grow with minimal exertion, freeing you from the endless grind and allowing you to focus on what truly matters in your life.

Passive income is more than just earning money while you sleep; it's an intentional shift in how you perceive and interact with wealth. At its core, it's about leveraging time, resources, and opportunities efficiently, so that your financial ecosystem becomes self-sustaining. With a strategic approach, passive income becomes a powerful tool, reducing the need for constant vigilance over your finances. It allows your earnings to amass and multiply, while you direct your energy towards passions and pursuits that fulfill you.

Before diving into creating passive income streams, it's essential to understand the assets and resources you already possess. Whether it's knowledge, skills, or investments, these existing elements can be harnessed to generate steady income. For instance, if you've got expertise in a particular field, writing a book or creating an online course can transform your knowledge into a long-term moneymaker. Real estate, dividends from stocks, or affiliate marketing can be avenues worth exploring, each requiring different levels of initial input but promising a rewarding output once set up.

Consider where your interests and values align with market opportunities. When your efforts are aligned with your passions, sustaining them over the long haul becomes a pleasure rather than a chore. Picture a hobby that's been more than a pastime—like woodworking or art—evolving into an online store, or a blog that shares your lifestyle insights turning into a source of affiliate income. Alignment of passion with financial growth ensures that the minimal effort you put in feels fulfilling, contributing not just to your bank account but to your personal sense of achievement.

Embarking on this journey requires a mindset shift from traditional models of earning. Instead of clocking in hours for dollars, the focus is on creating systems and structures that work for you in the background. Think of passive income as planting seeds; initial efforts are needed to ensure they take root, yet once they do, they grow and flourish with minimal interference. This shift in thinking not only nurtures your wealth but liberates your time, allowing you to simplify your life's complexities.

Let's dive into the simplicity of automation—the unsung hero of passive income. Setting up systems that automate processes can lighten your burden significantly. Whether it's scheduling blog posts, automating stock purchases, or using apps that manage and transfer funds, these resources can effectively manage aspects of your financial life with minimal oversight. Automation acts as a reliable assistant, assuring you that your financial interests are being handled efficiently.

There might be an initial learning curve, a slight discomfort that comes with stepping outside your financial comfort zone. However, embracing technology and digital tools can be your greatest ally. Use these resources to monitor, invest, and manage your income streams with ease, ensuring that your ongoing efforts are minimized while outcomes remain maximized. These systems create a sturdy framework within which your financial ventures can thrive.

However, it's crucial to stay informed and continually assess the health of your passive income streams. Regular check-ins ensure that what you've set up continues to serve your goals efficiently. Market trends shift, and new opportunities emerge, so staying adaptable and responsive to change is vital. Regular evaluation prevents stagnation and keeps your financial growth aligned with your life's broader objectives.

Flexibility and adaptability are not just complimentary strategies—they are necessities in maintaining sustainable passive income. The financial world is dynamic, and what works today may need tweaking tomorrow. Embrace a learning mindset, nurturing a keen awareness of evolving industry trends and emerging opportunities. Continuously refining your strategies ensures that your passive income streams remain a source of empowerment rather than constraint.

Imagine the peace of mind that comes from knowing your financial fortress is strong and self-sufficient. This state is attainable through cultivating a diverse portfolio of passive income streams, rather than relying on a single source. This diversity not only mitigates risks but also ensures that if one stream slows down, others continue to uphold your financial security. It's a way to safeguard against uncertainties, providing a resilient cushion that supports your minimalist lifestyle.

Passive income, when thoughtfully cultivated, becomes a testament to the power of minimalism in financial management. It reflects a lifestyle choice where less truly becomes more—more freedom, more time, and more opportunity to pursue the intangible wealth of life: relationships, experiences, and personal growth. This approach not only nurtures your financial health but enhances your overall well-being, allowing you to savor the richness of a life where wealth is plentiful yet requires little in the way of relentless striving.

As you embark on creating or enhancing your passive income streams, remember that the path requires patience, persistence, and a touch of creativity. The initial efforts invested might seem significant, but the long-term gains are profound. By carefully tending to your passive income garden, you ensure that it remains fruitful, continually contributing to both your financial stability and your life's simplicity. There's profound satisfaction in knowing that your wealth is working for you, empowering you to direct your energy towards the things that truly matter.

In sustaining wealth through minimal effort, you're not just accumulating money; you're crafting a deliberate life of simplicity and abundance. This journey promises freedom from the mundane tasks that once tethered your time, freeing you to immerse yourself in the joys of meaningful living. Through mindful cultivation, your dreams of financial self-sufficiency become not just attainable but enjoyable, a seamless weave of effort and ease.

Chapter 11: Financial Independence

Achieving financial independence isn't just about amassing wealth. It's about realizing that the freedom and security that come with it opens doors to choices you hadn't imagined. Imagine waking up and deciding how to spend your day—not because of obligation, but preference. This is the heart of financial independence: living life on your own terms.

To embark on this journey, it's crucial to plan for early retirement. This involves setting clear and measurable targets while adapting your lifestyle to meet those objectives. Set aside a percentage of your income with precision and consistency, always prioritizing your future self. It might seem daunting at first, but these small adjustments will compound over time, creating a powerful momentum toward your goal.

The FIRE (Financial Independence, Retire Early) movement is gaining traction as more individuals pursue this path. Understanding the movement means delving into its core principles: frugality, smart investing, and intentional living. While cutting expenses drastically to save more can be challenging, balancing this with maintaining the quality of life is essential. The journey to FIRE isn't a path you blindly follow—it's a tailored roadmap that aligns with your unique vision of happiness and freedom.

While the road to financial independence requires discipline and sacrifice, it's also an opportunity for profound personal growth. In shedding the layers of societal expectation, you gain clarity on what truly matters in your life. This insight becomes your guiding light, allowing you to align your actions with your authentic values.

In embracing financial independence, you're not just aiming for a future devoid of financial constraints. You're crafting a life filled with purpose, driven by intentional choices that reflect who you are and what you truly desire.

Planning for Early Retirement

Thinking about early retirement can be both thrilling and daunting. It represents a shift from the conventional timeline of work to something more personal and self-defined. Early retirement is more than a dream; it's a journey into embracing financial independence ahead of the traditional age. Before embarking on this path, it's important to understand the essence of this decision, which is a reflection of your values and the lifestyle you desire. At the heart of early retirement is the principle of financial freedom. This freedom allows you to choose how you want to spend your days, whether pursuing passions, volunteering, or traveling extensively. It's about taking control of your time rather than exchanging it for money. To achieve this, careful planning and a disciplined approach to finances become vital. The core of early retirement planning is not just about accumulating a significant sum of money, but also redefining your relationship with consumption and resources.

A common misconception is that only those who earn a substantial income can retire early. However, anyone can work towards early retirement by making intentional choices and prioritizing savings. Your income level is only one factor; the key lies in how you manage, save, and invest what you earn. Adopting a minimalist mindset can greatly aid in this process, allowing you to derive satisfaction from life by focusing on needs rather than wants, and by curating experiences over possessions.

Start by envisioning your post-retirement life. What does your ideal day look like? How important is travel, family, or hobbies? By creating a vivid image of your desired lifestyle, you align your current financial decisions with future goals. This vision acts as both a motivator and a guiding principle as you make sacrifices today for a more fulfilling tomorrow.

To reach early retirement, a robust and strategic savings plan is essential. Embrace a savings rate that pushes boundaries but remains sustainable for the long haul. For many, this might mean setting aside 50% or more of their income. While this might seem daunting, it's achievable by reducing living costs, cutting unnecessary expenses, and adopting a frugal yet rewarding lifestyle.

In tandem with saving, investing plays a crucial role. Investments are the engines that drive your savings to grow over time. It's not enough to just stash money into a savings account; you need a diversified portfolio that balances risk and reward. Learn about different investment options, whether stocks, bonds, or real estate, and find what fits your risk tolerance and timeline. The earlier you start, the more time your investments have to benefit from compounding growth.

Another critical aspect is healthcare, often overlooked in retirement planning. Health insurance becomes a major consideration, especially if you retire before qualifying for Medicare. Anticipate medical expenses and consider options like health savings accounts (HSAs) that offer tax advantages. Healthy living today can mitigate healthcare costs tomorrow, underlining the connection between lifestyle choices and financial planning.

Planning for early retirement also involves debt management. Carrying debt into retirement can significantly strain finances, as it often comes with interest rates that exceed potential investment returns. Make a robust debt elimination strategy part of your early retirement plan. Focus on paying off high-interest debts first and avoid accumulating new debts as much as possible.

Social security benefits, typically accessible at age 62, might not be in play for early retirees aiming for freedom in their 40s or 50s. Knowing this, your strategy should focus on building and withdrawing from personal retirement accounts, like Roth IRAs or 401(k)s strategically and intelligently. Understanding their tax implications and withdrawal limitations is crucial to avoiding penalties and optimizing income streams.

Lastly, consider the unexpected. Life is full of surprises, both good and bad. Building an emergency fund that covers at least six months of living expenses can offer peace of mind and a safety net. It safeguards against unforeseen expenses and provides stability, ensuring that a single setback doesn't derail your entire plan.

As you plan for early retirement, remember it's not a destination, but a journey—that requires continual adjustments and learning. Remain adaptable and open to reassessing your plans as your life circumstances and financial situation evolve. Success in early retirement planning is not just about the numerical figures, but also about the quality of life you are crafting for yourself. Let your personal values and aspirations guide this transformative phase.

Understanding the FIRE Movement

The pursuit of financial independence has taken many forms over the years, but none have resonated quite as powerfully as the FIRE movement. Standing for "Financial Independence, Retire Early," the FIRE movement encapsulates a lifestyle that blends disciplined saving and shrewd investing with the overarching aim of retiring far earlier than the traditional retirement age. For many, FIRE is not just a financial strategy, but a radical life philosophy that questions conventional norms about work and money.

The core idea behind FIRE involves maximizing savings by cutting down on unnecessary expenses, often paring lifestyles to what some might describe as the bare essentials. But don't mistake this for deprivation. Instead, it is a redirection of spending toward what truly matters to each individual. Whether it's freedom from the 9-to-5 grind, the ability to pursue personal passions, or simply more time with loved ones, FIRE emphasizes intentional decisions about where money goes, reflecting a mindset steeped in purpose and clarity.

To most effectively understand the FIRE movement, one must first grasp the principles that guide its followers. At the heart of FIRE is the calculation of one's "FI" number— Financial Independence number—essentially the amount of savings one needs to live off investment returns indefinitely. This requires a meticulous understanding of personal expenses and a laser-focused commitment to living within one's means. The next step involves investing the savings wisely, often in index funds and other low-cost investment vehicles to grow wealth over time.

However, the FIRE movement is not a one-size-fits-all approach. There are different flavors, or "sub-genres," if you will. Examples include Fat FIRE, Lean FIRE, Barista FIRE, and Coast FIRE, each accommodating varying levels of frugality, lifestyle comfort, and flexibility. Fat FIRE might appeal to those who wish to maintain a higher spending level in retirement, while Lean FIRE targets individuals willing to live more modestly. Barista FIRE allows for part-time work to supplement income, offering an appealing choice for those who want to balance work with more leisure. Finally, Coast FIRE refers to accumulating enough early in life that compounding interest will naturally grow the portfolio to support a desired lifestyle at a later age.

The movement's growing popularity can largely be attributed to its foundation on community and shared knowledge. Many adherents share their journeys online, providing insight and fostering motivation through blogs, podcasts, and forums. This collective exchange of ideas and experiences not only offers practical tips but also emboldens individuals to challenge traditional financial norms and societal pressures, creating a ripple effect that encourages broader participation.

Importantly, understanding the FIRE movement involves unpacking its psychological impact. The journey to financial independence often requires a dramatic mindset shift. It challenges one to move beyond material accumulation and toward a deeper connection with values and goals. This shift is not merely about accumulating assets but about redefining success and fulfillment outside of conventional boundaries. It's about making space for life's intangibles—like time, freedom, and personal growth.

It's crucial to approach the FIRE movement with a sense of balance and understanding of its potential challenges. Critics of the movement highlight the difficulty of maintaining such intense savings rates and the risk of unpredictable life changes. Additionally, there's the concern of what to do post-retirement when the structure and routine of a traditional job have disappeared. These are aspects that each participant must weigh and adapt to their unique circumstances.

No matter the path, a key takeaway from understanding the FIRE movement is the notion of control. Proponents of FIRE emphasize reclaiming control over one's time and financial future, free from the dependency on traditional employment. It's a movement that grants more than financial freedom, offering a profound opportunity to design a life more aligned with personal desires and less dictated by financial obligations.

Though the journey might seem daunting, the FIRE movement is inherently filled with optimism—a belief in one's ability to shape their destiny through calculated and intentional choices. The essence of the movement lies in aligning money with life's purpose, fostering a lifestyle where wealth supports personal goals rather than dictates them. As participants navigate their path to early retirement, they redefine what it means to live richly, not by material wealth but through the richness of experience and fulfillment.

The FIRE movement, while a beacon of inspiration, is also an invitation to consider and clarify one's financial philosophy. Understanding it prompts reflection on what money truly means in one's life, encouraging a conversation not just about retiring early but about living deliberately. Ultimately, it provides a roadmap for those who seek to enhance their life through financial independence, grounded in simplicity and personal empowerment.

Chapter 12: Practicing Gratitude and Contentment

Gratitude and contentment form the foundation of a minimalist approach to financial freedom. In a world constantly pushing for more—more possessions, more money, more status—finding joy in what we already have becomes a radical act. Practicing gratitude shifts our perspective, making us aware of the abundance around us, which in turn influences our financial decisions. This chapter delves into the transformative power of gratitude and how it can illuminate pathways to a simpler, more fulfilling financial life.

By consciously acknowledging and appreciating your financial blessings, be they meager or abundant, you create a mindset that's resilient against the incessant demands of consumer culture. You become more attuned to what truly matters, allowing for a natural reprioritization of goals. Consider adopting a gratitude journal specifically for your finances. Each day, jot down things you're thankful for in your financial life, whether it's a small savings milestone or the peace of mind that comes from having a budget. You'll find that this practice not only reduces stress and anxiety but also fosters contentment.

It's easy to fall into the trap of thinking that happiness lies just beyond the next purchase or pay raise. But contentment doesn't come from accumulating more wealth—it emerges from the richness of lived experiences and meaningful relationships. By embracing the minimalist philosophy, you learn to find fulfillment in simplicity. Think about the joys that cost little or nothing: time spent with loved ones, a well-prepared meal, or a quiet moment of reflection. These experiences provide a deep, lasting satisfaction that material wealth often can't replicate.

Ultimately, practicing gratitude and contentment requires a shift in mindset. It's about being present and acknowledging that what we have in this moment is enough. It's about finding balance in our lives and taking pride in the journey toward financial independence. When you cultivate gratitude, you open doors to a more enriched life, one where financial decisions align with your deepest values and aspirations. This approach doesn't just promise a secure financial future—it ensures that the journey there is joyful and fulfilling.

Cultivating a Grateful Financial Perspective

In a world where financial success is often measured by the size of one's bank account or the luxury of one's possessions, cultivating a grateful financial perspective can seem like swimming against the tide. Yet, the journey toward financial freedom isn't just about amassing wealth; it is equally about appreciating what you already have. Gratitude provides a powerful lens through which to view your financial situation, revealing not only the abundance that already exists but also the possibilities for greater fulfillment and peace of mind.

This perspective starts with an intentional shift in mindset. It involves recognizing and celebrating small victories that add up over time. These might be the moments when you successfully resisted an impulse buy or the satisfaction from tidying up your budgeting process. Each is a step toward a life where financial decisions are made out of confidence and contentment, rather than fear or scarcity.

Furthermore, by taking stock of the resources you already possess, you foster a sense of thankfulness that transforms your relationship with money. Reflecting on what you have, rather than fixating on what's missing, encourages gratitude. This can be a simple daily practice: perhaps listing what's in your pantry before deciding what's needed from the store, or recalling all the things a favorite pair of shoes has walked you through before considering a new purchase. These small acts of appreciation can shift your focus from lack to abundance.

Consider this: how often have you bought something only to find that the joy it brought was short-lived? When we practice gratitude, however, we begin to derive satisfaction from what we own by valuing its utility and beauty, rather than its novelty. This shift not only reduces superfluous spending but also builds a spirit of thankfulness, reducing the craving for more.

Building a grateful financial perspective also means recognizing that every financial situation presents opportunities, not just limitations. It's about understanding that financial well-being can stem not just from earning more, but from spending wisely and saving with purpose. A grateful heart sees potential in constraints, much like an artist sees potential in a blank canvas.

Even comparative simplicity can feel like a luxury when viewed through a lens of gratitude. By appreciating the simplicity of a home-cooked meal, a walk in the park, or the joy of a good book, you're investing in experiences that enrich your life without depleting your bank account. This is where gratitude meets contentment, creating a harmonious financial life that's about living with less but experiencing more.

Moreover, gratitude cultivates resilience. It's a tool that helps balance the ups and downs of financial life. In times of hardship, remembering past achievements and current assets can be incredibly reassuring, guiding you through turbulent times with a clear, focused mind. This resilience isn't just financial; it's emotional and mental, building a robust foundation for handling future financial challenges.

Gratitude can also deepen your sense of community and connection. By acknowledging the support and generosity of others in your life, you strengthen relationships, creating a network that can provide both financial and emotional support. Whether it's a mentor who offers advice or a friend who shares resources, these relationships are critical in creating a financially secure and fulfilling life.

Incorporating gratitude into your financial strategy doesn't happen overnight. It's a practice, one that you cultivate daily and reinforce through persistent effort. Start by making gratitude lists, reflecting on them regularly to see how your perception of your finances evolves. Celebrate milestones, no matter how small, and let them remind you of the progress you're making.

Use your financial journey as an opportunity to grow gratefulness and contentment, viewing each step not just as a task to check off but as a chance to recognize the wealth you already hold in your hands. Celebrate the freedoms you currently possess and the choices you're able to make, expanding your horizons and creating a life rich in both spirit and substance.

By cultivating gratitude in your financial life, you're not only aligning with a minimalist lifestyle but also fostering a sense of inner peace. This peace isn't dependent on market fluctuations or material possessions but grows from an appreciation for what's truly valuable—life itself. Embrace a grateful perspective, and you'll find that the quest for financial freedom becomes not merely a struggle or a chore but a rewarding journey in its own right.

Finding Fulfillment in Simplicity

In the midst of our hustle and bustle lives, the allure of simplicity is undeniable. This section delves into how a minimalist approach not only shapes our financial landscapes but also enriches our sense of fulfillment. Achieving this fulfillment doesn't require complex systems or grand acquisitions. Instead, it invites us to refocus on what we truly value—leading to profound satisfaction from the simple joys life offers.

The journey toward finding fulfillment in simplicity begins with introspection. It's about stepping back and evaluating what genuinely contributes to our happiness. When we strip away the excess and distractions, we're left with what truly matters. This isn't just an exercise in living with less. It's an enriching process of realigning our lives with our core values and removing the superficial layers that often cloud our judgment.

Consider the notion of owning less as a means to experience more. It's a powerful shift in thinking. Imagine your financial life free from the clutter of unnecessary expenses and obligations. With fewer distractions, it's easier to see and appreciate the wealth you already have, in financial terms and life itself. Freed from the constant noise of want, fulfillment naturally finds a place in the calm of simplicity.

Incorporating gratitude into this process enhances the journey even further. It's easy to take for granted what we have when distractions abound. By fostering a grateful mindset, we create space to appreciate the essentials and recognize their sufficiency. Gratitude becomes a tool for financial well-being and contentment, reminding us that fulfillment isn't tethered to the pursuit of more but found in appreciating enough.

However, the path to simplicity isn't a straightforward one. It requires confronting long-standing habits and societal pressures that equate success with abundance. Simplicity calls for courage to counter cultural norms and embrace priorities that nurture well-being over wealth accumulation. By recognizing that more doesn't always equate to better, we can focus on what truly enriches our lives.

Practical steps towards finding fulfillment in simplicity are diverse and adaptable. Start by evaluating your current spending habits and identifying areas for reduction without sacrificing comfort. This might mean canceling subscriptions you hardly use or reconsidering recurring purchases that don't add significant value to your life. Instead of buying for the sake of buying, weigh each purchase against its necessity and the joy it brings.

You can also foster fulfillment in simplicity by nurturing relationships and experiences over material possessions. Joy often resides in shared moments and cherished memories, not in things. Prioritize investing time and resources into connections with family and friends. Such engagements often yield richer returns than any possession could.

Additionally, simplifying your financial commitments opens up space for personal growth. With less financial burden, you gain the freedom to pursue your passions and hone skills that bring joy and sustenance. Whether it's taking up a long-neglected hobby, learning something new, or volunteering for a cause close to your heart, these pursuits enrich you in ways that transcend monetary value.

In essence, finding fulfillment through simplicity means reinterpreting wealth in broader terms. It involves a deeper appreciation of life's uncomplicated moments, whether it's the warmth of sunlight on your face, a walk in the park, or a quiet evening at home. It's about recognizing that these experiences, so easy to overlook in pursuit of 'more', are where true richness often lies.

The minimalist lifestyle presents challenges, but it also rewards with peace, clarity, and a profound sense of satisfaction. By committing to fewer distractions, we pave the way towards a life where authentic joy reflects in the simple, unadorned aspects of our existence. Financial freedom merges beautifully with deep contentment—a legacy of living fully and simply.

As you embrace this approach, clarity follows. Every decision, every purchase, every financial plan dovetails with your drive for fulfillment—not because you have more, but because you appreciate more deeply what you have. The beauty lies not just in the simplicity itself, but in the fulfillment and gratitude that unfold from within. Through this journey, you discover not just how to live minimally, but how to thrive profoundly.

Chapter 13: Minimalist Living for Families

Embracing minimalist living as a family might seem daunting at first. However, it opens up a world of opportunities for deeper connections and shared experiences. When everyone in the household is on board, it cultivates an environment where simplicity reigns over chaos, and intentionality trumps material accumulation. Children learn best by example, so simplifying your own life offers lessons that resonate far beyond words.

Start by engaging in open discussions as a family to understand everyone's needs and desires. What is truly essential? This collective pursuit anchors a family in values rather than things. Each member has a role, from choosing experiences over items to actively participating in decluttering spaces. Everyone's voice, including the youngest ones, should be heard when making significant changes. Creating a family budget plan isn't just about cutting costs but about aligning these financial decisions with your shared values. It reflects a commitment to prioritizing what truly matters.

A minimalist approach also means fostering financially savvy children. How can they save their pocket money or contribute to a small family goal? These early lessons are invaluable. When children see the tangible benefits of saving money for a family trip or a new shared experience, they understand the value of patience and planning. It's about teaching them to appreciate the payoff of delayed gratification, a lesson that will serve them well into adulthood.

With minimalism, the focus shifts from possessions to people. Family life thrives not on what you have but on who you're becoming together. Celebrate the small victories, like spending more time outdoors or enjoying game nights instead of screen time. These shared moments create a rich tapestry of memories that material goods could never replace. The journey to a minimalist lifestyle starts with small steps, but it's one that leads your family toward a meaningful existence marked by love, growth, and a shared vision of simplicity.

Raising Financially Savvy Children

In a world where consumerism is often cloaked in the guise of necessity, teaching children to navigate the financial landscape with wisdom is crucial. Minimalist living is not merely about having less; it's about making deliberate choices that reflect our deepest values. Imparting this philosophy to children weaves a financial foundation that is resilient, adaptable, and purpose-driven. It's about preparing them to confront financial complexities with simplicity and confidence. It begins with fostering an environment where mindful spending and saving become second nature rather than an imposed discipline.

Children are perceptive; they learn as much from what we do as from what we say. Demonstrating intentional spending habits can be a powerful teacher. When children witness a parent making purchasing decisions based on need rather than impulse, they learn discernment. It's an opportunity to involve them in the decision-making process, explaining why certain items are prioritized over others. For example, if a family is choosing to eat more homemade meals to save money for a meaningful vacation, explain this trade-off simply and clearly. It shows kids that financial decisions are about prioritizing long-term joy and goals over short-term gratification.

Another essential aspect is instilling an understanding and appreciation for saving. Encourage children to set goals for their savings, a process that can begin with something as simple as a piggy bank. Gradually, as they grow, introduce the concept of a savings account or investment in their name. This serves as a gentle introduction to the world of interest, dividends, and the idea of money growing over time. Instead of merely saving for a toy or gadget, suggest longer-term goals such as college savings or learning to invest in stocks. It makes the abstract idea of future planning more tangible and rewarding.

Financial challenges and opportunities often come disguised as everyday scenarios. Household chores or small tasks could be avenues to teach the value of earning and budgeting. It isn't about monetizing every action but about attaching real-world value to effort and contribution. Transparent conversations about family finances, tailored to age-appropriate understanding, can help demystify what money is and how it works. These dialogues need not be exhaustive or overwhelming but can build an understanding of what goes into earning, saving, and spending.

It also helps to provide children with tools to evaluate advertising critically. Teach them to recognize the difference between needs and wants, encouraging a mindset of gratitude for what they have. This doesn't mean shunning all desires but assessing them against the backdrop of their true happiness and long-term benefits. It's a skill that shields them from marketing ploys and societal pressures, promoting independence in decision-making. Similarly, celebrate experiences and time spent together over material possessions.

Furthermore, integrating lessons of generosity can enrich children's financial literacy in profound ways. Discuss the importance of giving, be it of time, talent, or resources, and how it fits within a minimalist mindset. Children can learn that sharing what they have enhances their community and leverages their privileges for common good. This outlook nurtures a sense of fulfillment and interconnectedness that transcends personal gain.

Education plays a crucial role in nurturing financial literacy. While schools may offer some level of financial education, don't rely solely on the institutional path. Incorporate financial literacy into daily life. Introduce them to foundational concepts like budgeting, taxes, and investment in incremental steps, ensuring they understand before moving to the next level. For instance, when planning a vacation or a big purchase, involve them in creating a budget. They'll see how decisions are guided by available resources and the pleasure of anticipating and fulfilling dreams sustainably.

Books, games, and simulations can significantly boost understanding and engagement. Consider age-appropriate literature that explains financial concepts in simple and enjoyable ways. Board games like Monopoly or online simulations where kids can practice scenarios of earning, spending, and saving are both educational and fun. These experiences offer practical lessons in handling finances, developing strategic thinking, and understanding economic transactions.

A minimalist approach to financial education advocates for patience. It's about teaching the virtue of waiting and working towards larger goals, resisting the urge for immediate gratification. Today's world makes it easy to indulge and spend, but conveying the rewards of patience and planning fosters a habit of thoughtful living. Sharing personal stories of when patience paid off can be motivational.

Ultimately, raising financially savvy children involves creating a legacy of self-reliance and thoughtful living. It empowers them to face life's uncertainties with a toolkit built on knowledge, discipline, and empathy. By cultivating these principles early on, we are not just preparing them to handle finances better, but we are also enabling them to lead lives rich in purpose and free from the burden of unnecessary material pursuits. It is about giving them the freedom to choose their path wisely, always guided by what truly matters. In doing so, we are crafting a future generation that carries forward the minimalist ethos in ways that will echo for years to come.

Creating a Family Budget Plan

When it comes to adopting a minimalist lifestyle with the goal of financial freedom, creating a family budget plan serves as a pivotal cornerstone. Crafting this plan doesn't just give you insight into your finances; it provides a roadmap for intentional living. By aligning your spending with your family's core values, you effectively turn a budget from just a spreadsheet into a tool for empowerment and simplicity.

Starting with a bird's-eye view is essential before diving into the nitty-gritty details. Take a moment to gather all your financial statements. This includes bank statements, bills, receipts, and any other documentation that sheds light on where the money goes. Understanding your income sources and regular expenses sets the stage for honest evaluations and meaningful conversations within the family. It's here that anyone, from the youngest child to the most reluctant adult, can join in discussing how their habits and choices impact the family's financial goals.

Next, you'll want to categorize your expenses. Consider using categories that resonate with your family's lifestyle, like "must-haves" and "nice-to-haves." Essentials such as mortgage or rent, utilities, and groceries naturally fall under "must-haves," while things like dining out, subscriptions, and entertainment might be considered "nice-to-haves." This step serves a dual purpose: it lays bare the reality of your current spending habits and identifies areas ripe for transformation.

Once you have a clear picture of your finances, it's time to involve the family in setting financial goals. Envisioning what you all truly want—from family vacations to future educational aspirations—infuses purpose into your budgeting efforts. Goals don't need to be confined to distant dreams. They can include short-term targets like switching to a cheaper phone plan or cooking at home more often. Each goal serves as a motivation, a tangible reason to rally together and track progress over time.

Creating a strict yet flexible budget template is crucial. Use tools like spreadsheets or budgeting apps, but make sure it's something the entire family feels comfortable accessing and updating. A successful family budget plan isn't one that feels like a noose around your neck. Instead, it's a living document that adjusts as circumstances change or as you achieve milestones. Set aside a specific evening each month to review the budget as a family—this ensures everyone remains committed and embraces accountability.

Conscious spending and saving should be woven into the fabric of your family's day-to-day life, not just seen as disciplines to comply with. Encouraging habits such as turning off lights when leaving a room or packing lunches may seem small but contribute significantly over time. At the same time, recognize and celebrate savings achievements—whether it's your first emergency fund milestone or successfully paying down a credit card.

It can be helpful to automate bills and savings to reduce stress and avoid pitfalls like late fees. By setting up automatic transfers to a designated savings account, not only do you prioritize savings, but you also remove the temptation of spending what you don't see. Automation doesn't mean losing touch with your budget; rather, it ensures that your minimalistic financial plan maintains its course while offering peace of mind.

Incorporating the family's shared values into your budget plan extends beyond just trimming expenses. Consider opting for experiences over material gifts. For birthdays or holidays, plan activities that create lasting memories and strengthen familial bonds.

Converting the effort into shared experiences emphasizes the joys of living with less yet gaining so much more in terms of family cohesion and happiness.

Revisit your budget plan at least once a year in a more comprehensive manner to include larger shifts in life circumstances, income, or major purchases. Perhaps you've decided to move, requiring a shift in housing expenses, or maybe you've welcomed a new family member and need to reallocate resources. Life is rich with change, and your family budget should evolve to reflect that.

One of the most enriching benefits of a family budget plan is that it teaches children financial literacy from a young age. Assign age-appropriate tasks, such as tracking allowance spending or comparing prices at the grocery store, to show them the value of money and the virtues of thoughtful spending. Such involvement not only contributes to the family process but also prepares them to become financially savvy adults.

Without overcomplicating things, a family budget that aligns with minimalist living principles transforms financial transparency into a familial cornerstone. It turns intentionality into a shared value and creates a narrative where every dollar spent reflects your collective priorities and dreams. It's a dynamic plan, one that adapts with your family, ensuring that financial simplicity can create an avenue not just for wealth, but for richer experiences and lasting fulfillment.

In the end, your family budget plan becomes more than just numbers on a page. It embodies a lifestyle where simplicity breeds both abundance and genuine contentment. By making mindful financial decisions together, you pave the way for a minimalist journey that everyone in the family can proudly share. And as you streamline your spending and focus on what truly matters, you become not just financial stewards but wise architects of a life well-lived.

Chapter 14: The Digital Minimalist Approach

In today's world, technology is both a blessing and a burden. It's streamlined our lives in many ways, yet also created complexities we never imagined. The digital minimalist approach, however, is about leveraging technology to do more with less. It's not about rejecting digital tools; rather, it's about using them strategically to simplify your financial life and foster intentional living.

Embracing a digital minimalist lifestyle doesn't mean cutting off your internet connection or deleting every app from your phone. Instead, it's about being selective with the tools and platforms you engage with. Start by identifying the technologies that genuinely add value to your financial journey. These are the apps and services that enhance your ability to track spending, manage investments, or automate savings without overwhelming you with information or distractions.

One key principle of digital minimalism is clarity. In a world besieged by notifications and alerts, clarity is power. Regularly audit your digital interactions to ensure they align with your financial goals. This might mean unsubscribing from marketing emails that tempt impulse buys or only using financial platforms that present data in a straightforward, comprehensible manner. Remember, just because you can keep up with every digital innovation doesn't mean you should.

Through a digital minimalist lens, we realize that less can indeed be more when it comes to technology and finance. Use technology to foster simplicity. Automated financial tools like budget apps or robo-advisors can relieve you of tedious tasks and free you to focus on more meaningful financial decisions. But avoid the trap of becoming a passive participant in your own financial life. Stay engaged and periodically reassess your tech stack to make sure it continues to serve your evolving needs.

Emphasizing intentionality extends beyond just financial management tools to encompass digital consumption as a whole. Be mindful of the time you spend online and how it impacts your financial decisions. Social media, for example, can be a double-edged sword. While it's a great place to gather tips and community support, it's also rife with influencers promoting lifestyles that may not align with your financial values. Cultivate a media diet that enriches, not distracts.

Finally, adopt the habit of digital decluttering. As with physical possessions, our digital lives can become cluttered with unnecessary subscriptions, apps, and accounts that no longer serve us. Regularly review and streamline these elements. Close inactive accounts, eliminate redundant apps, and tidy up digital files. This practice not only creates mental space but also can directly contribute to saving money by cutting out nonessential expenses.

By integrating the principles of digital minimalism into your financial strategy, you not only pave the way toward greater financial freedom but also create a lifestyle where technology supports rather than rules. Embrace digital tools as allies, not adversaries, and allow them to amplify the minimalist approach to your financial journey. With intentional use of technology, you can savor the benefits of modern advancements while living a life that's authentically aligned with your values. Through this balance, you'll find both peace and prosperity in a digitally driven world.

Utilizing Technology to Simplify Finances

In a world where technology permeates every aspect of our lives, crafting a financial life that blends simplicity with smart tech use is a path worth exploring. As digital footprints grow larger, the modern minimalist understands the power of technology in peeling back unnecessary complexities, ultimately creating space for what truly matters. Utilizing technology doesn't mean adding clutter but rather refining and enhancing our experience with our finances.

The first key to leveraging technology successfully for simplifying your finances is intentional selection and use of digital tools. Not every app or software out there is going to align with your minimalist goals. Begin by assessing what you need from these technological tools. Are you aiming for streamlined budgeting? Do you desire a clearer picture of investments or perhaps a more automated savings strategy? Identifying your primary objectives helps narrow down the vast sea of financial tech options to those that genuinely facilitate your minimalist financial journey.

Start with budgeting apps. These apps can transform the once onerous task of keeping track of expenses into a seamless experience. Many of these tools allow you to categorize your spending with minimal effort and provide a helicopter view of where your money goes. Apps like You Need a Budget (YNAB) or Mint help you synchronize your bank accounts to track spending automatically. The best part is, they eliminate the need for complex spreadsheets or inconsistent manual tracking.

Let's not overlook the powerful ally we have in automation. Automating bill payments and savings is an efficient way of decluttering your to-do list. When your savings contributions and essential bills are automated, it reduces mental load and gives you peace of mind. Your mind can then focus on strategizing the future, not just managing the immediate needs. In essence, automation discourages procrastination and encourages consistency, which is vital for financial discipline.

Banking online is another way technology simplifies financial management. Gone are the days of queuing up at a bank just to complete a transaction. Online banking platforms provide a wide range of services from fund transfers, mobile check deposits, access to statements, and even loan applications without having to leave the comfort of your home. Most banks offer mobile apps that alert you to transactions or balance changes—staying informed means taking control.

Investing, once reserved for those who could afford financial advisors, has democratized thanks to technology. With robo-advisors like Betterment or Wealthfront, you can invest money intelligently without needing extensive knowledge of the stock market. These platforms assess your financial goals and risk tolerance to create a diversified portfolio, often with lower fees than traditional advisors. By letting tech handle the heavy lifting, you spend less time managing your investments and more time on living.

Your financial data's security and privacy should remain a top priority as you explore digital tools. Choosing technology that employs robust security measures protects your life's earnings. Two-factor authentication, encrypted communications, and privacy settings are features you should insist upon. It's not just about accessibility but also about ensuring your data doesn't fall into the wrong hands. Having this peace of mind empowers you to use digital resources confidently.

Let's also give a nod to digital documentation systems. Storage apps like Evernote, Google Drive, or Dropbox ensure crucial documents are organized and within reach. By scanning and storing invoices, receipts, and important financial documents digitally, you not only declutter physical space but make them searchable and easier to retrieve. Time saved in finding these files can be invested in more meaningful activities.

Financial literacy evolves as new technologies emerge. Hence, staying informed about the latest tools and technologies in financial management should be a priority. Engage with communities or forums, attend webinars, or subscribe to newsletters dedicated to digital finances. Continuous learning ensures you're making the best use of technological advancements without feeling overwhelmed.

One of the understated yet significant roles of technology is its capacity to foster accountability. Personal finance apps often provide an overview of your financial landscape, serving as a visual reminder of where you stand relative to your financial goals. These visual aids can enhance motivation and keep you on track, much like a fitness tracker that nudges you towards your daily step goal.

More than just management, technology can influence your mindset towards money. It enables a financial strategy that's both structured and flexible. It helps you approach finances objectively, grounded in data and foresight, while allowing you to adapt and pivot when life's circumstances shift. This adaptability is a cornerstone of minimalist thinking, aligning perfectly with the pursuit of simplicity.

Finally, remember that while technology is a powerful tool, it's not an end in itself. It should always serve your broader purpose of achieving financial freedom through minimalist principles. Use technology to create space in your life, not fill it with more noise. The digital minimalist doesn't seek to own the most apps but rather to harness tools that enhance clarity, peace, and control over one's money.

By aligning technology with your financial intentions, you're not just simplifying your finances—you're reshaping how you live, work, and dream. The intersection of technology and minimalism is where true financial empowerment lies, inviting us to engage not in more but in less, and ultimately, in the best ways possible.

Managing Online Expenses Effectively

Embracing a digital minimalist lifestyle often leads us to reconsider the ways in which technology can either muddle or streamline our financial habits. In a world where our wallets have become virtual and transactions happen at the speed of light, keeping track of online expenses can feel like trying to hold water in your hands. But with the right strategies, it's entirely possible to manage these digital expenditures in a way that supports your journey toward financial freedom.

The first step in managing online expenses effectively is awareness. It's easy to lose track of spending when a simple tap or click seals the deal. Therefore, keeping an ongoing tally of your expenses is crucial. One way to maintain this vigilance is by using expense-tracking apps that integrate seamlessly with your bank accounts. These apps can automatically categorize your spending, giving you a bird's-eye view of where your money goes. Just as a garden thrives with regular tending, so does your financial life flourish with active stewardship.

Yet, as beneficial as technology can be, it's important to use it mindfully. Consider setting limits on your spending categories within these apps. By setting alerts, you'll be notified when you're nearing a threshold that you've set for yourself. This approach fosters intentionality, compelling you to weigh each purchase against your broader financial goals. These micro-decisions, seemingly trivial on their own, cumulatively steer your journey toward a life of abundance rather than scarcity.

Subscriptions can be silent saboteurs of financial plans, often set up and then forgotten. They continue to siphon money from accounts long after their usefulness has faded. Performing a regular audit of these recurring expenses is essential. Cancel any that no longer align with your priorities or offer true value. Challenge yourself to keep only those subscriptions that substantively enhance your life or contribute to your productivity and well-being. This will prevent unnecessary expenses from draining your resources.

Another effective tactic is to adopt a moment of pause before completing an online purchase. Just as mindful eating heightens awareness and appreciation for food, a pause cultivates mindfulness in spending. Before pressing "buy," step back and ask whether the purchase aligns with your current financial objectives. This brief contemplation can make all the difference between an impulse buy and an intentional acquisition. Over time, these mindful purchasing decisions reinforce the minimalist ethos of conscious consumption.

Digital minimalists also benefit from setting up automatic payments for essential, non-negotiable expenses. Automating recurring payments like utilities or rent can ensure you never miss a deadline, reducing stress and potentially avoiding late fees. Similarly, automated transfers toward savings or investment accounts can channel funds toward wealth-building endeavors right when you get paid, adhering to the principle of paying yourself first.

When it comes to managing online expenses, transparency within one's network of relationships can have a profound impact. Sharing financial goals and spending habits with a trusted partner or community can provide both support and accountability. Discuss your budgeting strategies, share tips on saving, and lean on each other when temptation strikes. This openness creates a shared vision and directs collective efforts towards enhancing financial well-being.

Moreover, adopting a minimalist approach can inspire creativity in handling digital expenses. Explore alternative solutions that don't involve spending money. Perhaps there's a community library that offers the digital services you crave, or a friend who's willing to lend you a rarely-used subscription in exchange for one of yours. This not only strengthens community bonds but ensures your financial resources are allocated toward more meaningful ends.

Finally, remember that this journey isn't about strict deprivation. It's about curating a digital financial landscape that sings in harmony with your values and aspirations. It might take time and adjustment, yet even small changes can yield significant results. By managing your online expenses with thoughtfulness and care, you actively shape a life that aligns with your desires, reinforcing that financial independence is within reach, without sacrificing joy or contentment in the present moment.

The beauty of the digital minimalist approach lies in its simplicity and adaptability. It empowers you to control technology, rather than allowing it to control you. As you continue on this path, let the guiding principles of mindfulness, intentionality, and creativity direct your digital financial habits. In doing so, you not only protect your financial well-being but also affirm your commitment to a lifestyle that honours both present satisfaction and future security.

Chapter 15: Minimalist Travel

Travel, in its essence, should be an enriching experience, free from the shackles of excess luggage and financial burdens. By embracing minimalist travel, we're not only cutting down on physical belongings but also adopting a mindset that prioritizes experiences over possessions. This approach encourages us to focus on the joy of discovery and the connections we forge with others, rather than the objects we acquire along the way.

Imagine packing for a trip with just one carry-on. It might sound daunting at first, but the freedom it affords is unmatched. With fewer items to manage, you experience less stress and more mobility. This method also aligns beautifully with financial prudence. The less we carry, the more we save—from avoiding baggage fees to not buying unnecessary travel accessories. Minimalist travel doesn't just lighten your luggage; it lightens the load on your wallet, too.

Moreover, traveling minimally helps us immerse ourselves in new cultures. When we aren't bogged down by our possessions, we're more open to learning from our surroundings. Choose to stay in local accommodations, enjoy street food instead of pricey restaurants, and use public transport. These choices don't just save money; they offer authentic glimpses into the lives of the locals, enhancing your travel narrative.

In the end, minimalist travel teaches an invaluable lesson: Life's true riches come from the landscapes we traverse and the people we meet. Experiences create lasting memories, far outlasting any souvenir. Remember, it's not about how much you see but how deeply you engage with each moment. On this journey toward financial freedom, traveling light can lead to a wealth of experiences, feeding both the soul and the bank account.

Making Travel Affordable and Enjoyable

Traveling, for many, resonates with freedom and discovery. It's an opportunity to escape daily routines and explore new sights and cultures. But what if we told you that travel could be both enriching and kind to your wallet? The secret lies in embracing minimalist travel, a philosophy that aligns beautifully with living a financially conscious life.

Minimalist travel begins with a shift in mindset. It encourages us to focus on experiences rather than possessions. This approach inherently makes travel more affordable. Instead of luxury accommodations or expensive mementos, find joy in local experiences and meaningful interactions. Imagine strolling through a vibrant market, tasting street foods, or having a conversation with a local artisan about their craft. These moments cost little yet offer immense value.

Planning plays a crucial role in making travel affordable. When you approach travel like a minimalist, you plan with intention and clarity. Set a budget that covers essential expenses while allowing room for spontaneity. Research is your friend here. Start by looking for flights well in advance. Use fare comparison tools and be flexible with your travel dates. Often, flying mid-week or during off-peak seasons can significantly reduce costs. Similarly, consider alternative accommodations like hostels, guesthouses, or even short-term vacation rentals that provide kitchens to cook your meals.

Speaking of meals, embracing local cuisine is another area where minimalist travel shines. It not only deepens your cultural experience but also trims down expenses. Dining like a local allows you to enjoy authentic dishes at a fraction of the cost of touristy restaurants. Plus, shopping at local markets can be an adventure. Preparing your meals gives you insight into the everyday life of your destination and keeps eating expenses to a minimum.

Consider transportation as well. Instead of renting a car, which can be a significant expense, explore the public transportation options available. Many cities have efficient and affordable bus, tram, or subway systems. Some places even offer the joy of exploration through biking or walking. Not only does this save money, but it also immerses you more deeply in the local environment.

Minimalist packers are wise travelers. Packing light reduces stress and eliminates unforeseen costs like airline baggage fees. Stick to versatile clothing that can be mixed and matched across multiple outings. Prioritize items that are multi-functional and durable. This practice reflects minimalist living and proves how less can indeed be more in enhancing travel enjoyment.

Moreover, one of the most enriching aspects of travel is forging connections. Volunteer opportunities, staying with a host family, or participating in local events often lead to the most memorable experiences. Not only do these activities often cost little or nothing, but they also provide a profound sense of engagement with the locale you're visiting. Through minimalism, you find that the wealth of travel is in the relationships you form and the lessons you learn.

Embrace the inevitability of surprises and snafus, a common occurrence on any trip. These moments, while initially stressful, often become the stories you cherish the most. Minimalist travel teaches adaptability and resilience, priceless skills that transform challenges into opportunities for learning and growth. When you travel with fewer expectations and more openness, you pave the way for richer experiences.

If you integrate these principles, you begin to see travel less as an escape and more as a thread woven into the fabric of your broader minimalist lifestyle. It becomes a vehicle for growth, connection, and, most importantly, joy. After all, the most fulfilling journeys aren't measured in miles but in memories. By making travel affordable, you make it accessible, ensuring it enriches rather than burdens your financial life.

The minimalist traveler realizes that just as in life, true wealth in travel isn't drawn from extravagance but from genuine interaction, discovery, and a conscious effort to tread lightly on both the earth and the pockets. Traveling with intention doesn't just make journeys more enjoyable—it makes them more meaningful. And through this approach, travel becomes not just a once-in-a-lifetime adventure but an ongoing possibility that continually enriches your life.

So, let your next journey be guided by minimalist principles. Focus on the essence of what travel offers rather than its illusions of decadence and luxury. Find beauty in simplicity and wonder in each moment. In doing so, travel will not only transform your perspective on the world but also align seamlessly with your journey towards financial freedom and intentional living.

Experiences Over Possessions

The essence of minimalist travel lies not just in packing light or choosing budget-friendly accommodations, but in prioritizing experiences over possessions. In a world where materialism often dictates success, taking a minimalist approach to travel encourages us to rethink what truly enriches our lives. By focusing on the experiences we gather rather than the souvenirs we collect, we tap into a deeper understanding of wealth—an understanding that aligns closely with the principles of financial freedom and intentional living.

Traveling with a minimalist mindset starts with the recognition that the memories and lessons we gain from our journeys are invaluable. When we choose to spend on experiences, we invest not just in fleeting pleasures, but in personal growth and transformation. A breathtaking sunrise from a mountain peak, an enriching conversation with a local, or the thrill of trying something completely new—these moments cannot be boxed and stored, yet they hold the power to shape who we are.

Imagine visiting a vibrant market in a foreign city. Here, rather than purchasing trinkets to display at home, engage with the people you meet. Ask vendors about their crafts, learn the history of the place, and taste the local delicacies. Such experiences offer insights far beyond material purchases, deepening your connection to the world and its diverse cultures. These are the memories that will stay with you, the stories you'll recount years later, fueling both nostalgia and inspiration.

Moreover, focusing on experiences can be surprisingly economical. While a minimalist traveler may forward funds toward a guided trek through picturesque landscapes rather than a luxurious five-star suite, the value derived from these choices often transcends mere cost. Such experiences craft richer narratives and provide a genuine sense of fulfillment, all while steering clear of financial strain. This shift in spending also fosters a profound gratitude for what we already possess, both in material and experiential forms.

Travel experiences have a unique way of prompting reflection. They challenge our preconceptions, broaden our worldview, and often remind us of the simplicity and beauty of everyday life. This introspection is crucial to minimalist travel, as it encourages gratitude and contentment—key elements of a minimalist lifestyle. By cherishing these moments, we find joy and fulfillment in things money can't buy, thereby aligning with the broader goal of simplifying our financial lives.

Beyond personal enrichment, experiences foster connections. Whether it's through shared adventures with family and friends or bonding with fellow travelers, these interactions can create lasting memories and meaningful relationships. This social aspect of travel, enriched by shared experiences, invokes a sense of community and belonging, reinforcing the idea that wealth is not just about personal gain, but about connecting with others in meaningful ways.

One critical consideration for minimalist travelers is the awareness of their environmental footprint. Experiences often encourage us to look for ways to immerse in nature responsibly and sustainably. This means opting for eco-friendly tours, supporting local economies, and minimizing waste. Such choices not only benefit the planet but also add depth to our travel stories. The realization that we're contributing positively to the places we visit enhances our travel experience, making it all the more rewarding.

As you explore the world with a minimalist mindset, you'll find that flexibility becomes a treasured companion. Minimalist travel sheds unnecessary burdens, enabling spontaneous decisions and allowing the journey to unfold organically. This freedom to adapt enriches the experience and opens doors to unexpected pleasures—be it stumbling upon a hidden gem or embarking on an unplanned adventure.

It's essential to remember that experiences over possessions extend beyond travel. This philosophy encourages us to embrace minimalism in all corners of life. By valuing moments and memories over items and attachments, we cultivate a life rich in purpose and meaning. We become more attuned to our true desires, aligning them with our financial goals and life values.

So, as you pack your bags for the next adventure, remember that every destination offers a tapestry of experiences waiting to be unraveled. Embrace the journey with open eyes and an open heart, for it is these experiences that will truly enrich your story, not the mementos you carry back. In the end, it is these intangible treasures that bring the greatest return on our investment in life.

With each trip, you refine your understanding of what you truly need to thrive. You learn to carry less but live more, focusing on the richness of experience over the weight of possessions. As minimalist travelers, embracing experiences not only enhances our journeys but also paves the way for a more fulfilling, simplified, and financially liberated life.

Chapter 16: Simplifying Your Home

Your home is more than just a shelter; it's a reflection of your values and lifestyle. Simplifying your home creates not only a more peaceful environment but also a more financially sound one. By clearing away the excess, you make room for what truly matters. You start to notice how much energy and resources go into maintaining a cluttered space. This realization can be transformative, leading to both mental clarity and financial freedom.

Imagine walking into a room where everything has a purpose and a place. There's a liberating feeling in knowing that each item supports your life goals. When you simplify your home, you redirect your focus from material possessions to life experiences. Minimalist spaces require fewer resources to maintain—less energy consumption, fewer repair costs, and generally less time spent cleaning and organizing. This shift doesn't just lighten the footprint of your home; it lifts a burden off your finances, freeing up resources for growth and enjoyment.

The process of home simplification can also enhance your financial decision-making. Practice intentionality by choosing quality over quantity for household items. It's not about restricting yourself to bare bones or living in deprivation. Instead, it's about enriching your environment with objects that offer value and function. This approach can lead to substantial savings as you're no longer investing in disposable trends or unnecessary gadgets.

Incorporating minimalism into your environment nurtures a more sustainable lifestyle that aligns with your financial goals. As you reduce the clutter and prioritize functionality and aesthetics, you find yourself living in a home that's not just simpler but also more meaningful. Your home becomes an ally in your journey toward financial freedom, encouraging a lifestyle that's intentional, appreciative, and focused on what truly counts.

The Financial Benefits of Minimalist Spaces

Turning your living space into a minimalist sanctuary isn't just about decluttering and aesthetics. It's a powerful step towards transforming your financial landscape, allowing you to save money, reduce stress, and create a more intentional living environment. In the heart of our busy modern lives, minimalist spaces offer a financial liberation that many of us seek but don't always know how to achieve.

First, there's the obvious benefit: spending less on stuff. When you decide to embrace a minimalist space, you're eliminating the constant need to fill it with unnecessary objects. This means fewer impulse buys and diminished consumer debt. You'll find yourself favoring quality over quantity, choosing items that truly enhance your life rather than temporarily satiate a want. Minimalism encourages you to focus on things you truly need, often leading to a significant reduction in overall expenditure.

Less physical clutter usually translates to a clearer mind. With a household that's easier to manage, you can focus on more essential financial tasks. You're not just decluttering your space; you're simplifying your financial decision-making process. There's a remarkable sense of liberation that comes when your personal space isn't filled to the brim with things vying for your attention. Minimalist environments foster clarity, helping you to make financial decisions that align with your long-term goals.

Beyond the apparent savings in purchases, simplified spaces can impact your utility costs. Consider the energy efficiency of a home without excessive possessions blocking light and ventilation. Fewer items mean fewer things to clean, which can lead to reduced energy use from appliances like vacuums and dishwashers. The ripple effect of a minimalist home also extends to maintenance costs. A sparse setting often results in fewer things breaking down or needing replacement.

Moreover, a smaller, well-organized home can lead to smaller living quarters. Many individuals seeking financial independence choose to downsize, embracing the increased affordability of smaller homes. Not only does this reduce mortgage or rent payments, but it can also lower property taxes, insurance premiums, and even costs associated with home improvement or renovation. Minimalist spaces encourage you to evaluate how much room you truly need to live comfortably, often uncovering significant savings in housing expenses.

Having fewer possessions doesn't just save you money; it can also generate income. By selling items you no longer need, you can simultaneously simplify your home and bolster your savings or utilize funds for other financial priorities. This decluttering process often reveals possessions you'd forgotten about—hidden gems that have the potential to add to your wealth or fund investments.

Messaging around minimalism frequently highlights its financial aspects, and for a good reason. The stress reduction associated with less clutter creates a cascade of benefits that seep into other areas of your financial life. Decluttered homes make for better environments to engage in productive activities, whether that's work-from-home situations or managing a side business. With this additional productivity, there's potential for increased earnings and further financial growth.

Furthermore, a minimalist lifestyle teaches resilience and adaptability. By learning to live with less, you train yourself to become resourceful, which can be a major asset in navigating economic uncertainties. Recognizing the non-material sources of happiness can lead to more conscious financial choices, prioritizing long-term satisfaction over temporary indulgence. This perspective shift is what ultimately fosters a wealth-centric mindset that appreciates experiences over possessions.

Embracing minimalist spaces is not just a temporary trend; it's a fundamental shift toward a more intentional and financially savvy way of living. It provides clear pathways to manage and multiply your financial resources, all while curating a home environment that supports well-being and mindful living. The financial benefits are significant, but they extend far beyond money, touching on improved quality of life and mental clarity.

In conclusion, transforming your home into a minimalist space doesn't just translate into a clutter-free living area; it unlocks a flowing current of financial opportunities. With less to maintain, purchase, and repair, a minimalist home can set the stage for true financial freedom. As you align your physical environment with your financial goals, you'll find an enriching synergy that propels you toward a more abundant and satisfying life.

Reducing Home-related Expenses

In our quest to simplify and achieve financial freedom, the home can often feel like both a sanctuary and a financial burden. Beyond its comforting walls lie numerous hidden expenses that quietly siphon away our resources. By understanding and reducing these home-related expenditures, we can achieve significant savings without sacrificing comfort or happiness.

First, let's consider the size of your living space. The allure of sprawling homes can be enticing, painted as symbols of success. But larger spaces often equate to larger bills—be it utilities, property taxes, or even maintenance costs. The minimalist approach asks you to reevaluate what you genuinely need to thrive. Could you downsize to a smaller, more manageable space? Doing so not only reduces direct costs but also encourages a simpler lifestyle with less clutter and complication. The fewer rooms you have, the fewer things you'll need to maintain and furnish.

Energy consumption stands out as one of the most significant home expenses. It feels deeply empowering to take control of our energy use, not just for the sake of our wallets but also for the environment. Start by investing in energy-efficient appliances and lighting. They might require a steeper initial outlay, but they significantly cut utility bills in the long run. Consider a programmable thermostat to optimize heating and cooling while you're away. Even simple acts like sealing windows or adding insulation can make a difference. On a brighter note, embracing natural light can drastically reduce electricity use. Rearrange your living space to bring in more sunlight. Over time, you'll notice a reduction in your electric bill as well as an improvement in your mood—a natural win-win.

Maintenance is another area where home-related expenses can easily spiral out of control. Regular upkeep, while seemingly costly, can stave off major repairs in the future. Create a routine maintenance schedule that includes tasks like cleaning gutters, checking HVAC systems, and inspecting roofs for wear and tear. By addressing small issues before they swell into significant problems, you'll save money and preserve your home's value.

When it comes to furnishing your home, question the necessity of each item. Do you need that designer couch, or could a second-hand option suffice? Scour thrift stores, estate sales, and online marketplaces for quality pieces with character. Meanwhile, explore DIY projects to breathe new life into tired furniture. These activities can be satisfying and memorable, and they're often more economical.

Let's not forget about water usage—a crucial aspect in minimizing costs. Installing low-flow showerheads and dual-flush toilets can halve your water consumption without sacrificing performance. Cultivate an awareness of how you use water: shorter showers, fixing leaky faucets, and running full loads in dishwashers and washing machines can contribute to sizeable savings over time.

Kitchen expenses deserve attention as well. It's tempting to dine out or stock up on convenience foods, but preparing meals at home is kinder to your wallet and often your health. Craft a meal plan each week to minimize waste and maximize ingredient use. Simple, wholesome meals can be savored and shared, reminding us of the beauty in simplicity. Additionally, maintaining a well-organized kitchen with only essential gadgets ensures you're not overspending on duplicate or unnecessary items.

Lastly, consider leveraging smart technology to monitor and optimize every corner of your home. From smart plugs to sophisticated home management systems, these tools can provide insights into your consumption patterns and highlight areas for improvement. While some systems may seem pricey upfront, they can lead to substantial savings down the line through efficiency and waste reduction.

It's an enriching experience to strip away the non-essentials and spotlight what truly contributes to your quality of life. By reducing home-related expenses thoughtfully and consistently, you're freeing financial resources to be channeled into what matters most: experiences, savings, or other life-enhancing investments. This journey towards a simpler, more intentional living situation is its own adventure—one that's deeply personal and uniquely fulfilling.

Chapter 17: Sustainable Financial Practices

In today's world, embracing sustainable financial practices isn't just a trend; it's a necessary part of creating a future-proof financial plan. By integrating environmentally conscious decisions into your financial life, you sustainably build wealth while contributing to the health of our planet. The foundation of sustainable finance is rooted in the principle of intentionality. Just like choosing a local, organic apple over a mass-produced one, each financial decision reflects your values and long-term goals.

Sustainable finance demands asking yourself, "How can my financial behaviors align with the environment and community's well-being?" This involves a deep dive into understanding where and how your money is invested. Are your investments supporting industries that align with a sustainable future? If not, it might be time for a little portfolio makeover. Seek out investments in green technologies, renewable energy, and socially responsible companies. These opportunities not only promise returns but also propel positive change.

Moreover, sustainable financial practices reach into our daily spending habits. Think of adopting an approach similar to a minimalist's wardrobe: buy less, choose wisely, and make it last. By prioritizing quality over quantity, you reduce waste and make purchases that last longer, ultimately saving money. Take stock of what you already own and mend it, repurpose it, or share it rather than replacing it. Simple practices like these lead to fewer financial outlays and less environmental impact.

Another facet of sustainable financial practices is minimizing waste in your budgeting process. By cutting down on unnecessary subscriptions and extravagant expenses, you not only save money but also reduce your environmental footprint. For instance, reconsider frequent car rides in favor of public transport, carpooling, or cycling. Such decisions significantly cut carbon emissions and often involve reduced costs.

Long-term sustainability in wealth building isn't just about preserving your finances but also growing them judiciously. Embrace the concept of "enough." When you understand what "enough" means for you, you naturally curb the urge to acquire more than you need, fostering contentment in both your heart and wallet. Your spending choices then start reflecting a conscious lifestyle, balancing today's delights with tomorrow's needs.

Furthermore, adopting sustainable fiscal habits isn't about perfection; it's about making progress. Begin by choosing one area of your finances to make more eco-friendly and gradually widen your efforts. Whether it's opting for a bank that invests in green initiatives or shopping at local farmers' markets, every small step counts. Don't underestimate the power of community when you're fostering these changes. Share your insights and learn from others, fostering an ecosystem of sustainable financial wisdom.

Ultimately, sustainable financial practices are a journey of aligning your personal wealth-building endeavors with broader ecological goals. As you continue on this path, you'll likely discover a more profound sense of purpose. This shift not only creates a healthier balance for your finances but also contributes to a sustainable world for future generations. And in that pursuit lies a ripple effect of change for both the planet and your pocketbook.

Environmentally Conscious Financial Decisions

In a world increasingly aware of its environmental challenges, making financial decisions with an ecological lens isn't just ethical but incredibly savvy. As the cost of natural resources rises and the impact of climate change becomes undeniable, adopting sustainable financial practices can simultaneously cushion your wallet and the planet. Whether you're an avid environmentalist or just getting your feet wet in this arena, the goal is to align your financial habits with ecological integrity.

Living an environmentally conscious financial life begins with a simple yet profound shift in mindset. It requires one to view financial decisions not merely as transactions affecting the immediate wallet but also as choices rippling through the broader ecosystem. For example, opting for renewable energy sources might seem like a higher upfront cost, but over time, this decision often results in significant savings on energy bills. Moreover, supporting clean energy companies contributes to a reduction in greenhouse gas emissions, thereby playing a small part in combating global climate change.

The concept of environmental responsibility extends to how and where we invest. Increasingly, investors are turning towards ESG (Environmental, Social, and Governance) investing. These investments not only provide the prospect of profitable returns but also ensure that one's money is supporting companies committed to sustainable practices. This requires research and sometimes a change in financial management strategies — considering funds that prioritize businesses with lower carbon footprints and ethical supply chains.

It's crucial to understand that environmentally conscious choices are often less about depriving yourself and more about re-evaluating priorities. Take, for instance, transportation. Relying less on gas-guzzling vehicles and more on public transport or cycling not only reduces personal carbon emissions but also slashes commuting costs. Similarly, investing in a fuel-efficient vehicle may seem costly at first, yet it can mean fantastic savings and long-term environmental benefits.

Incorporating sustainable practices doesn't stop at transportation; our homes can be sanctuaries of green living too. Energy-efficient appliances, better insulation, and water-saving technologies are investments that minimize utility expenses while contributing to environmental stewardship. These alterations reduce home energy consumption and, by extension, household costs. Additionally, choosing sustainable goods made from recycled or natural materials supports the green supply chain, encouraging the market to produce more eco-friendly products.

Food consumption is another area where financial decisions with an environmental focus can have substantial impacts. Embracing a diet that includes less meat can contribute to reduced demand for resources used in meat production, thereby conserving water and land. Additionally, purchasing locally sourced foods not only boosts local economies but also lessens the carbon footprint associated with transporting goods over long distances. Making a habit of buying seasonal produce can be cost-effective and beneficial for the environment, offering nutritious variety at a reduced environmental cost.

The notion of reducing waste within financial decisions can be equally transformative. Adopting minimalist practices in daily living can lead to less clutter, fewer unnecessary purchases, and a streamlined approach to spending. This extends to digital consumption as well — think before you print and consider digital options where possible. Such consciousness reduces paper waste, saves money on supplies, and is kinder to the planet's finite resources.

Recycling and reusing items instead of perpetuating the cycle of consumption can be financially savvy. Buying second-hand or refurbished goods saves you money and reduces demand on manufacturing markets, diminishing resource extraction and energy expenditure. Similarly, donating or selling items you no longer need enables you to reclaim space and occasionally garner some extra cash, all while supporting a circular economy.

We must recognize the role that our everyday habits and choices play in shaping the environmental landscape of tomorrow. For instance, consumer electronics can have devastating environmental impacts, leading one to consider the sources and the recyclability of these products. By opting for electronics with longer life spans or those made by companies with take-back programs, you're participating in a cycle that aims to lessen landfill burden and promote resource recovery.

Ultimately, environmentally conscious financial decisions weave practical benefits with profound ecological significance. They are about finding harmony between our financial imperatives and our ethical standings as stewards of the earth. While these decisions won't solve every financial or environmental problem overnight, they forge a path toward a sustainable future, demonstrating that what is good for the Earth can equally be good for our bank accounts.

Change manifests through actions as minor as choosing a reusable water bottle over single-use plastics or as major as investing in a solar panel for your home. Each decision is anchored in intentionality — considering both immediate outcomes and long-term effects. By embracing these choices, you align your financial practices not only with your personal goals but with a commitment to a healthier, more sustainable world.

Stepping into this realm involves some trial and error, but gradually, as these changes accrue, so do the financial and environmental rewards. Consider each dollar spent as a vote for the kind of world you want, and in doing so, you're not just changing your life, but becoming part of a larger movement committed to the planet's and posterity's well-being.

Long-term Sustainability in Wealth Building

Building wealth sustainably isn't just about accumulating assets or making savvy investments. It requires a long-term perspective that aligns with your values, embraces change, and focuses on the future. It's about fostering habits that ensure your financial health doesn't come at the expense of the planet or your peace of mind.

Think of sustainable wealth as an evolving garden. You sow seeds with clear intentions, nurture them regularly, and understand that growth takes time. You respect the seasonal changes and adjust your efforts accordingly, knowing that true abundance comes not from rushed efforts but from consistent, purposeful action over time.

Central to long-term sustainability is the principle of living within your means. This involves more than just budgeting; it's about being mindful of what you own and consume, and why. Many find that when they cut back to the essentials, they discover what truly brings joy and fulfillment. This shift from a consumption-focused mindset allows funds to be directed toward financial growth and stability.

Additionally, sustainable wealth involves making choices that benefit both your future self and future generations. Ask yourself, "How do my financial decisions today impact the wider world tomorrow?" For example, investing in companies with strong sustainability credentials not only supports positive change but can also offer enduring financial returns.

The concept of resilience is crucial in sustainable wealth building. Economies fluctuate, and so do personal circumstances. Preparing for uncertainties by building an emergency fund, diversifying income streams, and continually adapting your financial strategies can fortify your financial fortress against unforeseen events. It's about having the foresight to plan for different possibilities and the flexibility to pivot when necessary.

One practical approach to long-term wealth sustainability is to embrace intentional investments. This means not only seeking financial returns but also considering the ethical implications of investments. In recent years, impact investing has gained traction, where your financial capital supports ventures that aim for positive societal or environmental effects.

Moreover, sustainability in wealth isn't solely a financial concept. It intersects with the emotional and psychological aspects of living. It's about finding contentment with what you have while still aspiring for growth. This balance is nurtured by cultivating gratitude and contentment, which can prevent the elusive pursuit of excess wealth that often leads to stress and dissatisfaction.

As you focus on these elements, consider the power of education and continual learning. Staying informed about financial trends, emerging markets, or shifts in sustainable practices can enhance your ability to make well-rounded decisions. It's not necessarily about having all the answers but about asking the right questions that guide your path.

Further, incorporating minimalism can enhance the long-term sustainability of your wealth-building plan. Minimalism encourages you to strip away what doesn't serve you—be it financial products, possessions, or even relationships—and focus on what brings you value and joy. It creates clarity in decision-making and can illuminate the path to sustainable success.

But how do you measure success in sustainable wealth building? One indicator is the degree of freedom you experience—freedom to make choices that align with your values, to support causes you believe in, and to step back from work when required. Sustainable wealth is ultimately about independence and the freedom it grants to pursue life's pursuits with intention.

Engage with these concepts by setting clearly defined goals. What are your long-term aspirations? Perhaps it's retiring early, traveling the world, or ensuring your children's educational futures. By aligning these personal goals with your financial strategies, you create a roadmap that leads to a fulfilling and sustainable financial future.

Finally, consider the legacy you wish to leave. Think beyond the immediate impact of your financial decisions and ponder their long-term contributions to the world. By ensuring your wealth-building strategies embrace sustainability, you not only carve out a prosperous path for yourself but also foster an environment where future generations can thrive.

In summary, achieving long-term sustainability in wealth building requires a conscious, adaptive mindset that values both personal growth and broader societal impact. It asks you to be a steward of your financial resources, ensuring that your wealth supports not only your lifestyle but also the well-being of the planet and the community. Aim for growth that's slow but steady, mindful of your values and the broader world—because in this balance lies the true essence of sustainable wealth.

Chapter 18: Managing Economic Uncertainty

Living in a world that regularly shifts and changes means encountering economic ups and downs. No matter how well we've planned, the landscape can change, making uncertainty a part of life. Yet, rather than causing anxiety, this unpredictability can inspire a resilient mindset—one that turns challenges into opportunities.

It's crucial to start by equipping yourself with knowledge and awareness. You don't need to become an economic expert, but understanding the basic patterns and trends can help you anticipate potential challenges. Subscribing to reliable financial news sources or joining a community that discusses economic trends can keep you informed without overwhelming you with information. An informed perspective allows you to be proactive rather than reactive, a core principle in minimalist financial planning.

Preparing for potential downturns begins with building a robust emergency fund. This cushion isn't just a safety net; it's peace of mind. Ideally, your fund should cover three to six months of essential living expenses, tailored to your personal circumstances. By safeguarding essential funds, you create breathing space. You aren't only surviving during downturns; you're thriving, because your basic needs are secured.

Adaptability is another critical skill. Markets fluctuate, employment situations change, and expenses can shift. Embracing a minimalist mindset means being open to adjusting your budget and financial goals as needed. When faced with economic challenges, look to reduce or pause discretionary spending, and allocate those funds where they're needed most. Consider it an opportunity to reaffirm your financial priorities, focusing on what brings you true value and joy.

A diverse income stream can also be a valuable strategy in uncertain times. Relying solely on one source of income increases vulnerability, while having multiple channels softens the blow of any economic disruption. Whether it's a side gig, investments, or passive income opportunities, diversification can provide a safety net and ensure stability even during volatile times.

Beyond practical measures, nurturing an optimistic outlook is vital. Economic uncertainty often brings fear and doubt. Countering these emotions with hope and resilience can shift your energy towards creativity and problem-solving. Remember, resilience isn't about withstanding storms unbent; it's about how swiftly we bounce back, sometimes transformed and stronger.

Finally, fostering community relationships plays a crucial role. In times of economic pressure, relationships with family, friends, and neighbors can offer emotional support and resources. Communal sharing, services trades, and pooling resources can lessen the financial burden. Collective resilience emerges when people come together, harnessing the power of shared goals.

Managing economic uncertainty is not about predicting the future but preparing for it. It's about crafting a life that values essentials, embraces change, and sustains itself through mindful planning. Amid the shifting sands of economics, standing firm in your values and staying adaptable will guide you toward tranquility and confidence. It's about creating a life that remains simplified yet enriched, even as the world changes around you.

Overcoming Financial Challenges

Life's unpredictability often manifests itself in financial turbulence, whether through economic downturns or personal upheavals. It's in these trying times that overcoming financial challenges becomes not just an aspiration, but a necessity. Embracing a minimalist approach helps us anchor ourselves amid the chaos, guiding us toward decisions that shore up our financial resilience.

First, let's recognize that financial difficulties are universal. Everyone faces them at some point, so you're certainly not alone. The difference lies not in the occurrence, but in the response. Simplifying financial obligations helps mitigate the feeling of being overwhelmed. Start by identifying essentials versus wants. By eliminating non-essentials, your financial focus sharpens on what's crucial, reducing stress and freeing up resources for unexpected burdens.

Consider financial challenges as opportunities to reassess and strengthen financial strategies. This mindset shift transforms obstacles into stepping stones for growth. When confronted with a financial predicament, the goal should be to adapt quickly and effectively, gathering lessons and applying them creatively. Rather than viewing each challenge as a setback, it should be seen as a chance to thrive within a new framework of financial understanding.

Adapting a minimalist mindset can be instrumental in helping individuals navigate financial uncertainties. It encourages making clear distinctions between needs and desires, an approach that's crucial for maintaining financial health. This discernment aids in creating a suitable budget, one that is both sustainable and adaptable under shifting economic circumstances. When times are tough, the agility to scale back on non-essentials while preserving core necessities can make all the difference.

This adaptability should extend to income strategies as well. Consider diversifying income sources to buffer against potential financial shock. Whether it's through passive income opportunities, freelance engagements, or small entrepreneurial ventures, having multiple revenue streams is a prudent way to mitigate risks. This doesn't mean stretching oneself thin, but rather selectively amplifying skills that align with one's values and lifestyle.

Financial resilience also demands prudent cost management. During periods of economic uncertainty, practice heightened awareness with every financial decision. A methodical approach to spending, evaluating each expenditure for its necessity and alignment with long-term goals, conserves resources that might be needed in unforeseen scenarios. This can include critical analyzing of subscription services, habitual purchases, and discretionary spending.

Setting aside an emergency fund is another essential strategy. This financial cushion provides peace of mind and ensures you're prepared for life's surprises. Ideal amounts will vary based on individual circumstances, but a common benchmark suggests having three to six months' worth of essential expenses set aside. Building this fund gradually, with disciplined savings practices, is a testament to living minimally and intentionally. With each paycheck, earmark a modest portion for emergencies, reinforcing a prepared mindset over time.

During daunting financial times, staying informed but not overwhelmed is vital. When the broader economic landscape changes, be it through regulatory shifts or market fluctuations, sobriety in understanding these dynamics helps in crafting an appropriate response. However, be cautious of information overload, which can lead to anxiety. Curate sources of information and seek counsel from financial advisors who understand minimalist principles and your personal values.

Community can be a beacon when facing financial difficulties. Lean on networks and existing relationships for support, insights, and sometimes opportunities. Cultivating meaningful connections opens doors to shared resources and knowledge, alleviating some challenges of financial uncertainty. Collaborate with others who are also navigating the minimalist journey, sharing strategies and experiences to lighten the load.

Finally, practice resilience and patience. Financial recovery and growth take time, and often patience more than anything else. Acknowledge the journey as much as the destination, celebrating small victories along the way. This positive reinforcement sustains motivation and helps maintain focus on overarching financial goals despite immediate challenges.

By integrating these principles, overcoming financial challenges amid economic uncertainty transforms from a daunting task to a managed strategy. As you cultivate minimalism in all aspects of your financial life, these efforts yield peace, clarity, and resilience, enabling not just survival, but genuine growth and freedom.

Preparing for Economic Downturns

In today's fast-paced world, the sands of the economy are ever-shifting, and the tides of financial stability can change with little warning. It's important not to view potential economic downturns as mere storms to weather but as opportunities to strengthen our financial resilience. Preparing for these downturns isn't just about battening down the hatches; it's about building a foundation strong enough to withstand life's uncertainties. This section will guide you in crafting a robust and adaptable strategy for endure the economic fluctuations that are an inevitable part of life.

At its core, preparing for economic downturns is less about predicting the next financial crisis and more about establishing a lifestyle that can flex and adjust as needed. The forecasters may debate when the next recession will hit, but worrying about when is less productive than ensuring you're ready whenever it does. This involves cultivating a financial environment that's sustainable and adaptable—one that prioritizes values over valuables and needs over wants.

Begin by re-evaluating your expenses. This doesn't mean living in constant austerity but rather ensuring that every dollar you spend aligns with your priorities and values. When tough times come, a clear understanding of essential versus non-essential spending will provide the clarity needed to make quick financial decisions without the fog of panic. It's about creating a hierarchy of needs and wants, a conscious consumption ethos that will serve you well in any economic climate.

Next, let's talk about building financial buffers. An emergency fund might sound like old advice but think of it as a seasoned ally. It's there when unexpected expenses crop up like a flat tire on a rainy Monday morning—or when the market takes a nosedive. The goal is to have enough to cover three to six months' worth of living expenses. Consider this fund as your financial center of gravity—keeping you steady even when the world tilts.

Another key strategy is diversification. Often discussed in the context of investments, diversification is equally vital in your income streams. Think about how you can broaden your financial horizons. Whether it's developing side hustles, freelancing, or exploring passive income opportunities, having multiple sources of income can insulate you against the unpredictability of job markets. It's about weaving a safety net of opportunities that can catch you if one line frays.

Moreover, the skills you bring to the table are your financial lifeboat. Continuous learning and adaptability are non-negotiable in a world where job roles are rapidly evolving. Equip yourself with skills that not only augment your current career but also open doors to new avenues. In the face of economic downturns, your adaptability will be your greatest asset, easing transitions and facilitating resilience.

Let's not overlook the power of community. In times of economic strife, leaning on community networks can provide not only emotional support but also access to shared resources and collective wisdom. Building these connections now, during stable times, will ensure they are there to help you stay afloat when the waters get choppy.

Preparing for economic downturns also necessitates a reassessment of debt. Address any high-interest liabilities with urgency. Create a repayment plan that fits within your financial landscape. Minimizing debt means freeing up money that can be channeled into more flexible or rewarding ventures. High interest rates are an unnecessary strain on your resources, especially when you might need maximum flexibility.

Lastly, cultivating a mindset of gratitude and contentment plays an understated yet powerful role in financial resilience. Appreciating what you have curbs the perpetual chase for more, leaving you at peace with your current state, whatever it may be. This mental shift can shift your reaction to economic swings from fear to acceptance, seeing them as part of life's ebb and flow. Anchoring in contentment means that fewer things can shake your peace.

Ultimately, preparing for economic downturns isn't about fearing the future but embracing your ability to navigate it gracefully. It involves a deep understanding of your values, a flexible approach to income and spending, and a community that bolsters resilience. With these strategies, you're not just preparing to survive but setting the stage to thrive, no matter what the economic weather brings. When you enhance your financial resilience, you unlock the true freedom to live intentionally and with purpose, ready for what comes next.

Chapter 19: The Role of Health and Wellness

Living a life of financial freedom and simplicity isn't just about making smart investments or cutting expenses; it's about nurturing the foundation of it all—your health and wellness. Imagine your well-being as the cornerstone that supports a wealth-building lifestyle. When you prioritize your physical and mental health, you're better equipped to tackle financial challenges, make informed decisions, and savor the fruits of your minimalist journey. Good health can be a catalyst, powering your path to a more sustainable and enriched life.

Health and wellness have a strikingly synergistic relationship with financial well-being. When you're healthy, medical expenses dwindle, allowing more room in your budget for savings and investments. Consider it an investment in your future; money spent on quality food, exercise, and mental self-care pays dividends by reducing chronic health issues that can deplete your resources. Imagine the relief of fewer trips to the doctor's office, fewer prescriptions, and more funds available for things that enrich your life.

To achieve this, focus on financially efficient health strategies that align with minimalism. Instead of signing up for costly gym memberships, explore free or low-cost options like running, cycling, or body-weight exercises in nature. Tap into the bounty of seasonal and local produce, which is often more affordable and nutrient-dense than expensive, processed foods. With these approaches, you don't just save money; you also nourish your body with the right kind of fuel.

Remember, balance is key. While financial growth is crucial, it shouldn't come at the expense of your health. A harmonious balance between health and wealth not only amplifies success but also ensures the longevity of your minimalist lifestyle. After all, we can't enjoy financial freedom without the vitality to experience it fully. Let health and wellness be the bedrock upon which you build a life of simplicity and abundance.

Financially Efficient Health Strategies

As we delve into the intricate relationship between health and wealth, it becomes evident that they're inextricably intertwined. Embracing financially efficient health strategies not only nurtures our physical well-being but also plays a critical role in achieving financial freedom. By aligning our health choices with our financial goals, we create a sustainable model for holistic well-being and economic stability, reducing costs while enhancing life quality.

One of the fundamental principles of financially savvy health strategies is prevention. By prioritizing preventative care, we can significantly reduce the financial burden of medical expenses over time. Simple actions like regular exercise, a nutritious diet, and routine medical check-ups can prevent many serious health conditions. Investing time in these preventative measures might seem like a cost upfront but ultimately saves substantial amounts of money.

Nurturing a healthy lifestyle doesn't have to involve costly gym memberships or luxurious wellness retreats. Instead, explore options that fit a minimalist mindset. A brisk walk, a session of yoga at home, or a bike ride through a local park embodies the essence of health without financial drain. These activities not only enhance physical fitness but also foster mental clarity and emotional stability.

Our nutritional choices also significantly impact both health and finances. Preparing meals at home using seasonal and locally sourced ingredients supports both your body and your budget. Bulk cooking and meal prepping are practical strategies that minimize waste and ensure nutritious meals are always on hand. This approach also reduces the temptation to splurge on expensive, unhealthy take-out options.

Engaging with community-supported agriculture (CSA) programs or local farmers' markets not only encourages healthier eating but also costs less than purchasing imported exotic foods. Such choices define a minimalist lifestyle, emphasizing quality over quantity and supporting sustainable agriculture.

Moreover, understanding the body's nutritional needs can prevent over-reliance on supplements and vitamins, which can be surprisingly expensive and often unnecessary with a balanced diet. When supplements are needed, opting for essential, verified options ensures money isn't wasted on ineffective remedies.

However, our well-being extends beyond physical health; mental health is equally crucial and often overlooked in financial planning. It's important to be aware of the mental health resources available, many of which are free or low-cost. Public libraries, online platforms, and community centers offer various tools and support systems to maintain mental resilience.

Modern technology often provides access to affordable mental health resources. Mobile apps for meditation and stress management have become vital tools. Many of these are either free or offer budget-friendly subscriptions, providing alternative pathways to expensive therapy sessions and high-end wellness programs.

Another valuable strategy is investing in health insurance that meets your specific needs while being mindful of unnecessary add-ons. Understanding the details of your policy can prevent surprise expenses down the line. It's crucial to regularly review your coverage to ensure it aligns with your current health status and financial capability.

Furthermore, implementing a proactive approach to stress management can be a game-changer in maintaining both health and financial well-being. Chronic stress is often the root of various health issues, thus addressing it through strategies that don't require costly interventions is wise. Mindfulness practices or simple hobbies like gardening or reading can provide powerful stress relief without depleting finances.

The workplace offers another realm for financially efficient health strategies. Many employers provide wellness programs or incentives for participating in health-related activities. Taking advantage of these benefits not only improves health but also decreases healthcare costs and boosts productivity.

While it's essential to focus on personal health strategies, advocating for a healthier community can multiply these benefits. Community gardens, group exercise sessions, or local health workshops create a support system that empowers individuals and reduces costs. By sharing resources and knowledge, entire communities can thrive more affordably.

Lastly, remember that our choices today lay the foundation for long-term health. Setting aside funds for potential future health needs within a Health Savings Account (HSA) or Flexible Spending Account (FSA) provides peace of mind and financial preparedness. These accounts often provide tax advantages and can be crucial components of a comprehensive financial health plan.

These financially efficient health strategies showcase that living well doesn't require sacrificing one's savings or financial goals. By prioritizing and integrating health into our financial plans, we forge a path to an abundant and balanced life where health and wealth coexist harmoniously. As we strive toward financial freedom, it's crucial to recognize that each step towards better health is a step towards a more secure and prosperous future.

Balancing Health and Wealth

Let's dive into the nuanced dance between health and wealth, two critical components of a fulfilling, intentional life. As we strive for financial freedom through minimalist practices, it's vital to appreciate how our well-being and finances are intertwined. Prioritizing health doesn't just enhance your quality of life; it also safeguards your long-term financial prospects. Sounds compelling, right? Well, it's because a thriving mind and body often translate into a thriving wallet.

It's fascinating how often we overlook health until we're forced to confront it. Yet, by proactively nurturing our health, we lay the groundwork for sustained financial success. Think about it—the healthier you are, the less you'll spend on medical bills, treatments, and sick days. That's why, in our journey toward minimalism and financial independence, health must be a cornerstone.

Consider nutrition, which plays a pivotal role in our daily lives. Food isn't just fuel; it's an investment in your future. A well-balanced diet can ward off chronic diseases, reduce healthcare costs, and even boost productivity. It's about choosing whole foods—fruits, vegetables, lean proteins—not because they're trendy but because they nourish your core needs. By focusing on what adds true value to your body's ecosystem, you indirectly enrich your financial ecosystem as well.

Exercise follows closely behind. It's no secret that regular physical activity bolsters mental health and sharpens cognitive function. Engaging in movement—whether it's a brisk walk, a yoga session, or a swim—often provides the clarity and energy needed to tackle financial strategies with renewed vigor. Plus, many forms of exercise can be cost-effective or free, proving that you don't need extravagant gym memberships to stay fit.

Of course, sleep should not be neglected. Quality rest is crucial in maintaining both physical and financial acumen. During sleep, the brain processes information, repairs the body, and restores emotional balance. Compromising on sleep can lead to poor decision-making, impacting everything from daily finances to long-term investments. Make rest a non-negotiable part of your health and wealth strategy.

Now, shifting gears to stress management, it's undeniable that stress can wreak havoc on both health and financial stability. When we're stressed, we might indulge in impulsive buying, undercutting our savings plans. Moreover, stress often translates to health problems, which then spirals into additional costs. Techniques like mindfulness, meditation, or even journaling can do wonders for mitigating stress. Allocating time for these practices is a small price to pay for substantial mental and financial rewards.

The importance of preventive care can't be overstressed either. Regular health check-ups can flag potential issues before they become costly emergencies. Many minimalist philosophies emphasize getting ahead of financial mishaps by maintaining a solid financial plan; similarly, a proactive approach to health keeps future medical expenses manageable. Investing in preventive measures is akin to investing in a robust emergency fund for unforeseen life events.

An overlooked element in the health-wealth equation is the environment we create around us. Surround yourself with supportive relationships and communities that encourage a balanced approach to life. Engage in conversations about mutual financial goals and health tips. Often, wealth and wellness blossom in environments where there is mutual support and shared aspirations.

Finally, let's touch on mental health. While the minimalist journey can be deeply rewarding, it sometimes leads to introspection that might be overwhelming. It's essential to recognize when emotional support or professional guidance might be needed. Therapy and counseling are investments in your mental health that can pave the way for healthier financial habits and richer relationships.

In weaving together health and wealth, we align two pillars of resilience. A sound financial strategy rooted in minimalist principles inherently supports a healthier lifestyle. Similarly, prioritizing well-being enables sharper, more deliberate financial decisions. In this synergy lies not just the promise of wealth, but a life of genuine fulfillment and simplicity.

This balance isn't about perfection but about progression. As you forge forward, remember that the journey is profoundly personal. What works for one might not for another, and that's completely okay. The key is to continuously recalibrate, ensuring both health and wealth align with your values and long-term goals.

This chapter of your life is about recognizing that wealth isn't just a number but a holistic state where health and happiness multiply your riches. Embrace the journey, and let it lead to both peace of mind and prosperity.

Chapter 20: Time as a Financial Resource

Time is an asset more valuable than any financial resource, yet it's often overlooked in our modern hustle. Recognizing time as money isn't just a clever saying; it's a truth at the heart of achieving financial freedom. When we begin to see time as a finite resource that can bolster or impair our financial journey, our perspective shifts. We become more deliberate. Decisions about time start carrying the same weight as financial ones, requiring the same intentionality and minimalist principles we've applied to our spending and saving habits.

To truly harness time as a financial resource, it's essential to maximize its potential. This means mindful scheduling—prioritizing activities that align with both personal values and financial goals. Imagine the hours spent on an unnecessary purchase or a habit that drains rather than enriches. Now, envision reallocating that time toward learning a new skill, creating a side income, or simply enjoying moments that feed your spirit. The latter options not only enhance well-being but can significantly contribute to financial growth.

Minimalist living teaches us that less is indeed more, and the same applies to how we manage our time. By focusing on what truly matters, we reduce the clutter of endless commitments and obligations that don't serve our purposes. This approach offers mental clarity and creates opportunities for pursuits that bring both fulfillment and financial rewards. Remember, every minute saved from excess is a minute gained toward reaching your financial aspirations.

Time management isn't about filling every moment with busyness. It's about crafting a life where time works for you, not against you. Take the space to pause, reflect, and channel your time into avenues that will bring the most value. This intentional allocation of time can serve as a cornerstone of a minimalist financial strategy, enabling a freer, more prosperous life.

Maximizing Time for Financial Gain

When we think about wealth, our minds often gravitate towards money—what we earn, save, and invest. Yet time, that ever-fleeting and non-renewable resource, plays a crucial role in our financial landscapes. In the pursuit of financial freedom through simplified and intentional living, maximizing how we utilize time can greatly enhance our financial gain. Understanding this relationship requires not just a shift in mindset but a reimagining of our daily lives, aligning time spent with financial and life goals.

Time is often described as money for good reason. It is a resource that, when managed wisely, can lead to a plethora of opportunities for generating income and savings. However, the modern world, with its endless hustle and demands, often distracts us from this fact. By adopting a mindset that values time as a financial asset, you can unlock avenues of wealth that might otherwise remain hidden. Motivating ourselves to think of time management not as a chore but as a gateway to financial well-being is the first step.

One crucial way to maximize time for financial gain is through strategic planning. Just as you might map out a financial plan, creating a structured yet flexible schedule allows you to allocate time effectively to activities that contribute to your financial goals. Whether it's dedicating an hour a day to learning a skill that could boost your income, or setting aside time for research into investment opportunities, these intentional actions build toward a more prosperous future.

Moreover, an often underestimated aspect of maximizing time for financial gain lies in multitasking efficiently. Combining compatible activities can optimize your schedule without overwhelming your mental bandwidth. For instance, listening to finance-related podcasts while on a jog not only benefits your physical health but also enhances your financial literacy. This synergy between tasks fosters a productive use of time, bringing you closer to your financial aspirations.

However, it's also essential to recognize the limits of multitasking. Not all activities pair well together, and understanding when to focus solely on one task can be equally beneficial. Deep, uninterrupted focus, known as deep work, emerges as a potent tool for achieving substantial progress—whether you're building a side business or tackling a complex financial problem. The value of concentrated attention cannot be overstated, as it allows for higher quality outcomes and fosters innovation.

There's also power in the small moments. Micro-steps, or brief bursts of activity strategically aligned with your financial goals, can cumulatively lead to significant outcomes. Think of these snippets of time—five minutes here to review your budget, ten minutes there to set a new saving target—as compound interest: small actions building on each other, generating exponential growth. Embracing these moments for the high-value potential they hold turns potentially wasted time into tangible financial benefits.

In modern life, distractions are rampant and relentless. Emails, social media notifications, and the ever-alluring internet can derail even the most disciplined among us. Addressing these distractions head-on and creating digital boundaries can liberate valuable time for productive endeavors. Limiting screen time, scheduling focused internet usage, and applying tools like website blockers are practical strategies to reclaim time from the digital realm for your financial gain.

Practicing mindfulness can also aid in balancing time and financial goals. When you are fully present in your activities, you are more likely to complete them efficiently and find satisfaction in the process. This approach not only reduces stress but allows for better decision-making regarding financial matters. By being mindful of how you spend your time, you naturally cultivate habits that prioritize tasks aligned with your financial goals.

Equally important is resting and recharging. Overworking can lead to burnout, rendering any time management plan unsustainable in the long term. As paradoxical as it may seem, scheduled downtime becomes a strategic investment. Allowing yourself time to unwind, reflect, and reset enriches your subsequent efforts, replenishing your energy for the tasks that propel you toward financial independence.

Delegation merits special mention when maximizing time for financial gain. Identifying tasks that can be outsourced—not just domestically but also professionally—frees up your time for high-value activities. This strategy requires trust and investment but ultimately extends your capacity to focus on what matters most. Whether it's employing a financial advisor or leveraging virtual assistants, effective delegation magnifies the impact of your time.

Lastly, let's talk about the transformative power of community in maximizing time. By engaging with like-minded individuals, you can leverage their knowledge and experiences, expediting your journey towards financial goals. Participating in groups dedicated to financial literacy or investment opportunities not only provides education and motivation but also holds you accountable, ensuring your time is spent wisely and goals are met efficiently.

In essence, maximizing time for financial gain involves a disciplined approach where clarity of purpose and a commitment to minimalism intersect. By appreciating time as an invaluable financial resource, the journey to financial freedom becomes not just attainable but abundant with potential. Shifting your perspective on how time influences financial outcomes empowers you to craft a life that is as financially rich as it is fulfilling.

So, as you strive to simplify your financial life and grow wealth, remember that your time is as valuable as any other asset in your portfolio. Manage it with the care and attention it deserves, and the financial gains will surely follow.

Time Management for a Minimalist Lifestyle

In the fast-paced world we're living in, it's easy to lose track of time. Days blur into one another, and before you know it, weeks have passed, and goals remain unfulfilled. This relentless march of time can become overwhelming, especially when there's a constant allure of endless choices and distractions. But for those who embrace minimalism, time becomes more than just the ticking hands of a clock; it transforms into a precious financial resource. When we manage our time well, it has the potential to amplify our wealth and simplify our lives, allowing us to align our actions with our financial values. The key is to transform how we view and utilize time.

Minimalism and time management go hand-in-hand, almost like a perfectly choreographed dance. By focusing on what truly matters, both in our personal and financial lives, we can cut through the noise of unimportant tasks. This approach helps us direct energy to activities that yield the most value. For instance, if managing investments provides long-term financial security, then dedicating time daily or weekly to assess one's financial portfolio becomes invaluable. The minimalist principle of essentialism guides us to classify tasks into what is genuinely important versus what can be forgone or delayed.

Every day, each individual is blessed with 24 hours—a true financial goldmine once you recognize its potential. By setting clear priorities and focusing on high-impact tasks, the minimalist approaches time much like they approach finances: with intention and clarity. It's akin to clearing clutter from a room; only the essentials remain, offering clarity and serenity. Yet, this isn't about rigid scheduling; it's about making the present moment count, where every tick of the clock brings us closer to our aspirations.

To manage time effectively within a minimalist framework, the first step is acknowledging our daily patterns and habits. Start by tracing your activities throughout the day. Which tasks consume the most time, and are they contributing to your financial and personal growth? This self-awareness is a bridge to understanding where shifts need to be made. Often, this exercise reveals not a lack of time, but an inefficient allocation. By reframing how we view these blocks of time, we can begin to see them as sections to be enhanced, not just managed.

Constructing a minimalist daily schedule isn't about filling hours with tasks but ensuring that the tasks we choose are the right ones. The principle of "less is more" echoes here. By removing tasks that don't align with a bigger financial or personal purpose, we free up time to manage resources more efficiently. Think of it as "budgeting" your time similarly to how you'd budget finances. Allocating minutes or hours to activities that promise the best returns—be those returns emotional, financial, or otherwise—is pivotal.

There's an unparalleled satisfaction found in being present, a cornerstone tenet of minimalism. When each moment is appreciated and utilized wisely, life becomes richer. This doesn't mean every moment needs to be productive in the traditional sense; sometimes, the most valuable use of time might be resting or reflecting. These moments allow our minds to recharge, leading to greater creativity and efficiency when focusing on more demanding tasks. Essentially, in the minimalist's toolkit, rest is as crucial as action.

It's essential to consider the quality over the quantity of time spent. The modern world often equates busyness with productivity. However, for the minimalist, the measure of success isn't how much you do, but how well you do it and how aligned your actions are with your core values. As financial activities often demand focus and precision, minimizing distractions becomes crucial. By using techniques such as digital decluttering, you can maintain a workspace—both physical and mental—that encourages deep work.

The decision to say 'no' becomes a valuable tool in every minimalist's arsenal. Detaching from non-essential commitments and activities creates space for time to be invested more meaningfully. This doesn't just apply to obvious time-wasters but also to engagements that may once have been important but no longer serve your core goals. This amended schedule clears paths, opening up more substantial blocks of time that can be applied toward advancing a minimalist financial strategy.

Mindfulness practices can further reinforce the minimalist's time management approach. By staying grounded and actively present in each task, you fortify your focus. Meditation or deep-breathing exercises serve as reminders of the moment, providing clarity and increasing overall productivity. Such practices not only enhance contentment but also have tangible effects on efficiency, proving that sometimes the path to doing more is to first pause and reflect.

Time management for minimalists also involves scrutinizing recurring tasks and automating where possible. By setting up financial machines, such as automatic bill payments or investment contributions, invaluable time is saved, allowing it to be redirected towards strategy and growth. These small tweaks, while seemingly insignificant, compound over time, freeing up hours and mental bandwidth for more constructive pursuits.

The minimalist's view of time is an enlightened one—it's not merely measured in hours but in moments of impact. Aligning actions, thoughts, and time with one's values requires discipline but offers priceless dividends. As you align your time like you would a balanced financial statement, remember that wealth isn't just the accumulation of material goods but also mastery over one's life choices.

Ultimately, mastering time as a minimalist propels us toward not only financial success but personal fulfillment. Through intentional living and disciplined time management, we achieve a life of abundance, free from the clutter of excess—truly gold for those of us seeking financial freedom through simplicity. With each step taken and each decision made, we're not just saving time or managing it; we're enriching it, moment by moment.

Chapter 21: Navigating Social Pressures

Living a minimalist lifestyle often means confronting social pressures that challenge our financial choices. At first glance, it might seem daunting—friends and family may not understand why you're skipping the latest gadget or fancy dinner. The key here is to remain steadfast in your commitment to a simpler life. Remember, minimalism is a personal journey that prioritizes well-being over material status.

When friends suggest yet another shopping spree, it's an opportunity to lead by example. Share how minimalism has not only decluttered your space but also enriched your life experiences. You don't have to preach, but a simple testament to the peace and freedom you feel can be inspiring. It often opens the door for conversations that may encourage others to rethink their own financial priorities.

Developing a strong sense of self-awareness is crucial when navigating these pressures. Recognize your triggers in social settings that may push you toward unwanted spending. It could be a group of peers who equate success with the latest possessions, or family who views financial generosity as love. Once you identify these, focus on setting clear boundaries. A polite "no" can respect both your values and your relationships.

Sometimes, addressing social pressures means finding community in like-minded individuals who share your values. Seek out groups or forums dedicated to minimalist living, where you can exchange ideas and support each other. By surrounding yourself with people who encourage intentional living, you'll find your resolve strengthened and your social interactions more fulfilling.

Ultimately, navigating social pressures requires both empathy and determination. Understand that not everyone will appreciate your minimalist choices, and that's okay. Stay true to your path by remembering why you chose this lifestyle in the first place—financial freedom and a richer life experience that's not defined by possessions. When you uphold your minimalist values in social settings, you're reinforcing your commitment to a life of intention and purpose.

Maintaining Minimalist Values in Social Settings
Navigating social settings while holding true to minimalist values can be a delicate dance. Friends and family often influence our spending habits more than we might like to admit. While socializing, the pressure to conform by way of spending — be it for dinner at trendy restaurants or the latest tech gadgets — is ever present. It can be especially challenging when everyone around seems to equate happiness with material wealth. However, staying grounded in minimalist values in these situations is not just possible, it's empowering.
Creating a mindset that prioritizes personal values over societal expectations is the first step. This doesn't mean completely abstaining from social activities, but rather approaching them with intentionality. Sometimes it's as simple as suggesting or hosting more budget-friendly get-togethers. Imagine the joy found in a potluck evening with friends, where everyone contributes a dish, cutting down on costs without compromising on enjoyment. Such events remind us that true joy is found in human connection, not in excessive spending.
When faced with an invitation to an event or an expensive dinner, pause and evaluate. Ask yourself, "Will this bring genuine joy and value to my life?" This assessment helps in distinguishing between what we do out of love and genuine interest versus what we do out of social obligation. By filtering your engagements through this lens, you spend both time and money only on what truly matters to you, reinforcing your minimalist values.
It can be helpful to communicate your lifestyle choices to your peers. Many people shy away from discussing financial or lifestyle commitments due to perceived judgments or misunderstandings. However, transparency can foster mutual understanding. You may even find that your minimalist choices inspire others to simplify their own lives. Being open about why you might not choose to attend every single event or why the latest fashion craze doesn't appeal to you helps others see that it's a deliberate choice, not a limitation.
Despite our best efforts, there will be times when we encounter unwelcome pressures. A friend might encourage a lavish purchase with the best intentions, thinking it'll lead to happiness. In these moments, it's crucial to lean on the inner strength cultivated by a minimalist mindset. Remember, minimalism is about removing excess to make room for the meaningful. By consistently aligning actions with values, you establish personal integrity that resists external pressures to conform.
A support system can be invaluable when maintaining minimalist values in social settings. Surround yourself with like-minded individuals who respect and understand your lifestyle. Consider joining groups or forums focused on minimalism and wealth-building. Here, you'll find encouragement, advice, and camaraderie, while sharing your own experiences and insights can reinforce your commitment to a minimalist lifestyle.
Moreover, reframing social experiences through the lens of minimalism opens up new perspectives. Look for opportunities to connect that don't involve spending — a walk in a park, a shared hobby, or an at-home movie night. These alternatives emphasize experiences and connections rather than material consumption and can be far more fulfilling in the long run. Doing so also gently shifts the dynamic of social engagements from consumption to shared experiences and exploration.
Resisting the urge to become entangled in social competition is a key facet of maintaining minimalist values. It's not uncommon to find social situations infused with subtle

competitions around who has the biggest house or the latest gadget. In these instances, take a moment to appreciate the comfort that minimalism provides. Embrace a mindset where peace and fulfillment are derived from simplicity, quality, and purpose rather than quantity.

Kindness and generosity are intrinsic aspects of social interactions. With a minimalist approach, you can express these without breaking the bank. Small but significant acts of kindness, like lending an ear, offering help, or sharing resources, go a long way and are often more genuinely appreciated than material gifts. Such behavior reinforces the notion that you value relationships over commodities.

When encountering skepticism or criticism regarding minimalist choices, remember the why behind your lifestyle. Understand that skepticism often stems from misunderstanding or discomfort with simplicity, which stands in stark contrast to consumer-driven norms. Sharing the benefits you've gained — the peace, freedom, and focus on intentional living — can help others see value in what might initially seem unconventional. If handled tactfully, these conversations may even plant the seeds of change in someone else's life.

Your minimalist values should evolve as you journey through life, gaining experience and wisdom. Each interaction and social event offers an opportunity to refine these values. Your social circle can be a testing ground for these values, allowing you to adapt them as necessary. Remember, minimalism isn't a rigid framework but a flexible guide that adjusts to your changing circumstances and deepening understanding of what truly matters.

Leading by example can have a significant and unforeseen impact. By consistently maintaining minimalist values, you showcase the peace, freedom, and contentment achievable without succumbing to societal pressures. Your approach to life can inspire others to adopt a more intentional lifestyle. You may find that over time, you develop a community around shared values, reinforcing your commitment to minimalism and perhaps simplifying your social interactions even further.

Ultimately, preserving minimalist values in social settings revolves around intentional living, prioritizing meaningful experiences, and genuine connections over fleeting conveniences. Surround yourself with supportive individuals, remain transparent about your lifestyle choices, and constantly re-evaluate the meaningfulness of social engagements. Through mindful navigation of social pressures, you create a life that aligns with your minimalist and financially savvy values, encouraging those around you to do the same.

Overcoming External Financial Expectations

Navigating the labyrinth of social expectations can feel like a relentless dance, constantly pulling you in different directions. At the intersection of society's whispers and our own desires, lies a critical path to financial freedom. It's a journey that begins with understanding and ultimately overcoming the external financial expectations that often tether us, pulling us away from our minimalist ideals.

Social pressures can manifest in myriad ways, from the subtle hints of friends about joining the latest vacation trend to more overt forms like family expectations to maintain a certain lifestyle. These pressures often come packaged in well-meaning advice or cultural norms that, on the surface, appear innocuous but can have profound effects on our financial choices. The challenge is not just to recognize these influences but to navigate them with an intentional and minimalist mindset.

Start by observing the areas in your life where external expectations weigh the heaviest. It could be in the realm of fashion, where trends come and go at a dizzying pace; or perhaps in social gatherings, where status symbols are worn as badges of honor. Recognize that these pressures are largely external metrics imposed upon you. They are not inherently tied to your personal value or success, despite what society might indicate.

As you journey towards financial minimalism, redefine what success means to you. This process involves an introspective look at your values and aligning them with your financial actions. Success shouldn't be gauged by the scale of your possessions or the facade of wealth. Instead, it's about living a life rich in experiences and free from unnecessary constraints. By defining these terms on your own, you are less likely to feel the tug of external expectations.

Consider the role of communication in overcoming these social pressures. Often, friends and family may not be aware of your financial goals or the minimalist path you're embracing. Open, honest conversations can help set boundaries and manage expectations. Share your journey and your reasons for making the choices you have. This transparency not only helps others understand your perspective but might also inspire them to reflect on their financial habits.

While conversations are powerful, living out your values is equally impactful. Your actions—committing to a minimalist lifestyle despite societal nudges—speak volumes. By consistently making choices that align with your values, you reinforce your own commitment and gradually influence those around you. The ripple effect of living authentically can encourage others to re-evaluate the financial norms they've always followed without question.

There will always be instances where societal pressures seem insurmountable. That's where community comes into play. Surround yourself with like-minded individuals who share similar values. This support system can provide encouragement, accountability, and innovative ideas to stay committed to the minimalist path. Whether it's joining a minimalist group or an online forum, fostering connections with folks who understand your perspectives can be invaluable.

In the pursuit of financial minimalism, it's crucial to differentiate between personal desires and societal expectations. Sometimes, what we think we want is a reflection of what society deems necessary for approval and acceptance. This discernment requires mindfulness.

Practicing regular self-check-ins on your motivations for purchases or lifestyle choices can help you stay true to yourself.

It's also worthwhile to reflect on the consequences of succumbing to external pressures. Understand the long-term impacts these choices can have on both your finances and overall well-being. Acting against your own financial principles to meet external standards often leads to stress, anxiety, and a detachment from the things that genuinely bring joy and fulfillment.

To effectively counter these pressures, develop a strong financial plan rooted in your values. This roadmap acts as both a guide and a shield. It's a tangible affirmation of your journey towards intentional living and financial freedom. Review this plan frequently, allowing it to adapt as you grow and encounter new situations, so it always resonates with your core values.

Moreover, embracing gratitude and contentment serves as an antidote to external pressures. Appreciating the abundance you already possess shifts focus away from societal benchmarks towards more personal, meaningful parameters. Take time to savor the simplicity and autonomy of your choices, cherishing experiences and relationships over physical possessions.

In essence, overcoming external financial expectations is not about rejection but about intentional redirection. It's a continuing process of aligning your financial actions with your intrinsic values and remaining steadfast in your pursuit of a minimalist lifestyle. By doing so, you'll find yourself not just sailing through the waves of societal pressures, but mastering them with grace and conviction.

Remember, the aim is not perfection but progress. Celebrate each small victory in maintaining your minimalist choices, knowing that each step taken is a testament to your resilience against external pressures. In the grand tapestry of life, those who dare to forge their own paths often find the greatest fulfillment waiting quietly at journey's end.

Chapter 22: Leveraging Community and Relationships

Community and relationships play a crucial role in the journey toward financial freedom, offering an often overlooked source of strength and inspiration. While financial strategies can feel like a solitary path, standing together with like-minded individuals transforms the journey, unlocking collective wisdom and shared enthusiasm. Imagine not just building a network, but a true cadre of supporters, each member sharing experiences, challenges, and victories.

In these networks, mutual support becomes an invaluable resource. The power of sharing experiences involves more than exchanging advice; it's about learning from diverse perspectives and avoiding pitfalls that others have encountered. People who've faced similar situations can provide insights on navigating complex financial decisions, offering practical tips that textbooks may overlook. Collective intelligence flourishes, and what was once daunting becomes manageable through collaboration.

Building financial support networks extends beyond professional circles. Friends and family, often our closest confidants, can encourage healthier financial habits or even embark on joint ventures to achieve common financial goals. Whether it's a small investment club or a larger community initiative, pooling resources and talents can yield exponential benefits. Besides material support, emotional encouragement from loved ones can be an anchor, particularly during times of uncertainty.

Shared knowledge is a crucial aspect of leveraging community ties. Organizing workshops or attending seminars can foster an environment where open conversations about financial health are normalized and destigmatized. Through this transparency, you learn not only from success stories but also from painful financial lessons others have faced. These conversations reinforce that financial growth is an ongoing journey, not a destination.

As you build relationships rooted in shared values and goals, you also strengthen your financial resilience. These connections don't just support immediate objectives; they enrich the entire journey toward wealth. Walking this path arm-in-arm, learning and growing together, isn't just motivational — it's transformative.

Building Financial Support Networks

The journey to financial freedom is not one to be taken alone. It thrives in the company of others, blossoming when nurtured by a community that understands and shares its values. In the realm of intentional living and financial minimalism, building a network that offers both support and wisdom can be transformative. It's about connecting with those who inspire, challenge, and hold you accountable to your financial aspirations while you're doing the same for them.

Creating a financial support network begins with openness. Start by having candid conversations about money with those you trust. It could be family members, friends, or even colleagues who share a similar financial philosophy. These discussions can help break down taboos surrounding money matters and encourage a culture of transparency. You might be surprised by how many people are eager to share their experiences and learn from others. When financial conversations become the norm, they lose their stigma, leading to collective empowerment.

Variety in the network enriches the experience. Include people with diverse backgrounds and experiences, as each can offer unique insights. Someone may excel at budgeting, another in investing, while someone else might have mastered the art of living well within their means. This diversity ensures that all aspects of financial well-being are covered, and each member can both contribute to and benefit from the collective knowledge. Align yourself with individuals who are driven to achieve financial simplicity, so the foundation of your network remains strong and purposeful.

Don't hesitate to seek out organized groups or communities focused on financial support and education. Online forums, local meetups, and social media groups dedicated to minimalism or financial independence are excellent places to engage with like-minded individuals. These digital and physical spaces not only magnify the possibilities for connection but also expand the horizon for learning. Engaging with a larger community can provide access to mentors, potential collaborators, and even friends who've walked a similar path.

Reciprocity is key to sustaining a robust financial support network. As much as you gain from others, it's essential to give back. Share your own experiences, the successes, and the hurdles. Your insights might become the catalyst for someone else's journey. Offer encouragement, celebrate milestones together, and lend support during setbacks. This exchange forms a network that's not just transactional but also deeply communal and supportive.

Inspiration can strike in the most unexpected places, and often the people who surround you play a pivotal role in that process. You may not realize it immediately, but each interaction within your network has the potential to sculpt your financial perspectives. Whether it's someone questioning your spending habits or suggesting a resource you've not yet considered, these interactions often lead to breakthrough moments that drive progress.

Build a network that challenges you. Friends or mentors who push you to clarify your financial goals can help you stay focused. Holding each other accountable can serve as a formidable motivator in adhering to established financial frameworks. When the journey seems daunting, knowing that there's an entire network backing you can make all the difference.

Another invaluable aspect of a support network is the sharing of resources and opportunities. In practical terms, this might look like pooling resources for bulk buying, sharing tools, or even housing accommodations. Over time, such practices can much reduce expenses, contributing to collective financial health. Additionally, knowledge-sharing about new technologies, investment opportunities, or budgeting hacks can lead to breakthroughs that might have been elusive otherwise.

As the network grows, introduce structured activities that reinforce financial wellness. These could be monthly meetings to discuss progress, workshops on essential financial skills, or collaborative challenges. Some might appreciate a virtual book club focusing on financial literature, while others might schedule regular check-ins to ensure everyone stays aligned with their financial goals. These activities not only strengthen the bonds within the network but also maintain an actively engaged community.

It's important to remember that financial support networks are not static; they evolve. As your financial journey progresses, so will the dynamics of your network. Some members may come and go, and the focus might shift based on collective needs. Embrace these changes, as they reflect growth and adaptation, essential components of both minimalist and financial philosophies. Be open to new members and fresh perspectives, which will invariably enrich the tapestry of experiences within the group.

Ultimately, the networks we build are reflections of our values and aspirations. By cultivating a strong financial support network, you're not just enhancing your own journey toward financial freedom; you're contributing to a larger movement of intentional living. Together, you create a vibrant ecosystem where shared knowledge turns into shared strength, and in that strength lies the prowess to transform lives—yours, and those around you.

Sharing Resources and Knowledge

At the heart of every community lies a robust network of support, built on a foundation of shared resources and knowledge. The ancient art of collective living shows us how pooling resources can elevate individuals and neighborhoods alike. In today's fast-paced world, tapping into these timeless practices can be a boon for those pursuing financial freedom through minimalism.

Imagine you're setting out on a new financial journey. Instead of going it alone, you decide to join forces with others who share similar goals. This approach doesn't just lighten the burden; it enlivens the experience with camaraderie and shared wisdom. It's about leaning on each other and making life's journey more manageable and enjoyable.

One of the key ways to share resources is through community swaps and lending libraries. These initiatives, often grassroots in nature, enable us to circulate goods, tools, and even skills without the need for money. By borrowing instead of buying, you save money and foster a spirit of trust and cooperation in your community. Imagine a library where, instead of books, you borrow gardening tools, kitchen appliances, or even camping gear. The possibilities are endless.

Knowledge-sharing extends far beyond tangible resources. Whether it's a skill or an insight, sharing what you know can make a profound impact on someone's financial journey. Consider the power of community workshops and classes. These gatherings can cover a wide array of topics, from basic budgeting techniques to more advanced investment strategies. By attending or even leading a session, you have the chance to learn something new or reinforce your own understanding.

The digital age has ushered in new ways to share information and resources, giving rise to online communities that cross geographical boundaries. Platforms such as forums, social media groups, or even apps designed for financial literacy allow people to connect over shared interests and goals. These communities offer guidance, support, and the collective wisdom of their members, creating a virtual village where you can ask questions, share solutions, and celebrate each other's milestones.

Meanwhile, local community gardens exemplify both resource and knowledge sharing. While they obviously provide fresh produce, they also offer an educational opportunity. Experienced gardeners can share their know-how with novices, fostering a sense of unity and empowerment. Planting and tending a garden teach patience and respect for the natural pace of growth—principles that readily translate to financial habits.

Time-banking is another powerful concept that's gaining traction. In a time bank, hours are the currency, and everyone's time is valued equally. If you spend an hour walking someone's dog, you earn an hour's credit which you can use to receive a service, like a guitar lesson or having someone help you with grocery shopping. Time banks recognize the inherent value in all skills and encourage a community-building mindset.

Storytelling is an often-overlooked yet vital component of knowledge sharing. Personal narratives that reveal financial mistakes or triumphs can serve as cautionary tales or roadmaps for others. By sharing your story, you might illuminate a path for someone else, encouraging them to avoid certain pitfalls or to explore new avenues. Remember, transparency breeds trust—and in a cohesive community, trust is indispensable.

Moreover, partnerships with financial experts or local businesses can unfold new educational opportunities within communities. These partnerships might involve weekly seminars, casual meetups for financial advice, or even collaborative platforms for buying groceries in bulk at discounted rates. Often, financial institutions offer free workshops, covering topics ranging from home-buying basics to retirement planning, eager to support community knowledge as it fosters customer loyalty.

Sharing resources and knowledge requires an openness and a readiness to trust. It demands that we look outward, redefining our relationships with our neighbors and broadening the scope of community. By adopting this mindset, we create an environment where knowledge flows freely, and resources are abundant—even in their simplicity.

Financial mentorship is another aspect worth considering. Those who have successfully navigated their financial paths often feel a sense of duty to offer guidance to others. As a mentor, you can provide tailored advice, helping someone to plot their own course toward financial security. This practice not only enriches your mentee but also continuously renews your own understanding and commitment.

The ripple effect of collective efforts in resource and knowledge sharing can be transformational. When individuals come together, a culture of abundance forms even within the framework of minimalism. Collective success bolsters that of the individual, creating cycles of empowerment and resilience.

Ultimately, by embracing the principles of sharing, you become a part of something bigger than yourself. You connect more deeply to others, enriching your own life and those of your community. This synthesis of sharing and solidarity can make the pursuit of financial freedom a joyous and sustainable journey.

Chapter 23: Continuous Learning and Adaptation

In our ever-evolving financial landscape, the ability to continuously learn and adapt is crucial for anyone seeking financial freedom through intentional living. While the principles of minimalism provide a strong foundation, staying informed and flexible allows you to enhance your strategies and respond effectively to changes. It's not enough to set your financial plans on autopilot; you need an eye on the horizon, ready to make adjustments as needed.

Continuous learning isn't just about absorbing new information—it's about cultivating curiosity and a willingness to evolve. The financial world is like a living organism, constantly changing with technological advances, economic shifts, and societal transformations. Embracing a mindset of lifelong learning ensures you're equipped to navigate these changes with confidence. Subscribe to trusted financial newsletters, follow insightful blogs, and engage with thought leaders who challenge your perspectives. In doing so, you open yourself up to a world of knowledge that can enhance your financial journey.

Adaptation, on the other hand, is your response to the insights gained through learning. For many, adaptation can seem daunting, primarily if it involves letting go of long-held beliefs. Yet, it's within this flexibility that financial resilience thrives. Consider how you might adjust your investment portfolio in response to emerging market trends or how you could reallocate resources to support new financial goals. The key is to remain agile and open-minded, recognizing that change, though often unsettling, is a powerful catalyst for growth.

An integral part of adapting successfully is self-reflection. Regularly evaluate your financial strategies to ensure they align with your life values and changing circumstances. Ask yourself whether your current approach still serves your broader life goals, or if perhaps it needs a fine-tune. This practice of mindful reflection not only aligns with minimalist principles but also fosters a deeper sense of satisfaction and control over your financial destiny.

Moreover, learning and adaptation aren't solitary endeavors. Engaging with a community of like-minded individuals can provide fresh perspectives and collective wisdom. Whether through financially-focused online forums or local meetups, surrounding yourself with others who share your values amplifies your understanding and ability to adapt. These relationships offer support and challenge, helping you see beyond your own experiences to adopt more diverse, well-rounded strategies.

In embracing continuous learning and adaptation, you empower yourself to not only navigate the present but to anticipate and thrive in the future. While the road to financial freedom is unique for everyone, the commitment to grow, evolve, and learn ensures that you're always moving forward. This commitment transforms potential setbacks into valuable lessons and opportunities for progress.

Staying Informed About Financial Trends

In the ever-evolving landscape of finance, staying informed isn't just a wise choice; it's a necessity for anyone seeking financial freedom through a simplified and intentional lifestyle. The world of finance can often feel overwhelming, shrouded in constant change and complex jargon. However, with the right tools and mindset, you can navigate these waters with confidence, ensuring that your financial strategies remain relevant and effective.

Let's start with understanding why it's crucial to keep an eye on financial trends. Financial trends are like the changing seasons of the economy; they bring shifts that can impact your wealth-building journey significantly. Just as a gardener observes the weather to nurture their plants best, being aware of these trends allows you to make informed decisions about saving, investing, and spending. It's not about chasing every trend but recognizing the ones that align with your minimalist approach to wealth.

The digital age has redefined how we access information, which means the barriers to staying informed are lower than ever. With a myriad of tools at your fingertips, embracing the digital sphere is less about technology and more about how you can leverage it to stay ahead. Online platforms, financial news websites, and even social media come alive with insights and developments that could influence your economic decisions. Each of these platforms provides a diverse range of perspectives, allowing you to look beyond traditional narratives and find information that resonates with your financial ethos.

One of the most valuable habits you can cultivate is setting aside dedicated time to review financial news. It's akin to practicing mindfulness; you're turning your awareness towards something that directly impacts your future. Whether it's once a week or a daily ritual, find a rhythm that complements your lifestyle without adding stress. Opt for sources that have consistently provided you with accurate and beneficial information, and don't shy away from exploring new voices in the financial sphere.

However, staying informed isn't just about passive consumption of information; it's also about engaging with it. Question the insights you gather and consider how they fit within your personal financial goals. Engage in discussions, whether online or within your social circles, to expand your understanding and challenge existing beliefs. Often, these conversations lead to new insights and reinforce the adaptive mindset crucial for thriving in a rapidly changing financial world.

While the financial landscape is constantly shifting, certain fundamental principles remain steadfast. Economic cycles, for instance, have persisted throughout history. A thorough understanding of these cycles can be immensely beneficial. Knowing the signs of an impending recession or recognizing a booming market can guide you in making decisions that bolster your financial stability rather than compromise it. By familiarizing yourself with these patterns, you equip yourself with a time-tested strategy to buffer against uncertainty.

It's equally important to pay attention to the sociopolitical factors that can influence financial trends. Policy changes, trade agreements, and shifts in government leadership are just a few examples. These elements can ripple across the economy, impacting everything from interest rates to employment levels. While you can't control these dynamics, staying informed allows you to anticipate potential impacts and make proactive adjustments to your financial plan.

Another dimension of staying informed involves recognizing the interplay between global events and personal finance. We live in an interconnected world where a crisis or breakthrough in one nation can reverberate around the globe. Understanding how these global events might influence your financial reality can prevent you from being caught off guard. Whether it's commodity price fluctuations or emerging technologies disrupting traditional markets, the global stage plays a significant role in shaping financial trends.

To adopt a truly minimalist approach to finance, focus on quality information rather than quantity. Amidst the noise, discernment can be your greatest ally. Set clear criteria for what qualifies as relevant news. Think of it like curating a capsule wardrobe; each piece should be versatile and purposeful. In this way, each piece of financial information should serve a function in your broader economic strategy.

Don't forget the power of networking with financial professionals and enthusiasts. Engaging with these communities, whether through seminars, webinars, or casual meetups, can provide fresh insights and different perspectives. Financial experts not only offer industry-specific knowledge but also practical advice gleaned from years of experience. By listening and sharing, you become part of a collective learning process that enriches your understanding while building support networks.

Moreover, consider feedback a vital component of your financial journey. Leaders and learners alike benefit from constructive feedback, so don't hesitate to reflect on your approach regularly. Are there gaps in your knowledge that could be addressed by seeking more targeted financial education? Are your sources diverse enough to provide a balanced view? By asking these questions, you're embracing a cycle of continuous improvement that keeps your financial strategies dynamic and robust.

In moments of doubt or when overwhelmed by information, remember that staying informed is less about memorizing every detail and more about understanding the broader narrative. Focus on trends that align with your financial objectives and lifestyle values. With consistency and clarity, the changing tides of finance become less intimidating and more of a participant in your journey toward financial freedom.

Finally, ground yourself in gratitude as you navigate the financial landscape. Staying informed empowers you to make choices that are not only financially sound but also meaningful. It's about investing your time and energy into practices that resonate with your values, and in turn, crafting a financial narrative that supports a life of simplicity and intentionality. In the end, being informed is about much more than accumulating wealth; it's about enriching your life with purpose and peace of mind.

Evolving Your Financial Strategy

Financial strategies aren't set in stone. Like a garden thriving under tender care, they grow, adapt, and sometimes require pruning. In the realm of finance, stagnation is often the harbinger of obsolescence. To build wealth and simplify our financial lives, it's essential to cultivate a mindset of continuous evolution. By doing this, we stay resilient and agile, two qualities that hold immense value in both the financial world and our personal lives.

Adaptation begins with awareness and curiosity. Ask yourself: What new financial tools could simplify my life? It's crucial not to shy away from changing outdated methods. For example, utilizing apps that automate savings or investments can save time and reduce the likelihood of oversight. Technology is our ally in this modern age, empowering us with tools to make financially sound decisions without overcomplicating our lives.

A responsive strategy isn't just about numbers and data; it's about aligning your financial actions with your current values and circumstances. Flexibility allows you to adjust your approach as life unfolds. Consider this a journey rather than a destination. As your priorities shift, your strategy should reflect those changes. Whether it's a change in career, a new addition to the family, or a decision to embrace minimalist living even more deeply—your financial plan should bend like a willow, not break like an oak.

Your goals serve as guiding stars in this financial evolution. Envision them as fluid rather than rigid, permitting room for refinement. This vision isn't just about altering dollar amounts but re-evaluating what wealth truly means to you. Is it the freedom to travel? The security of a comfortable retirement? Or perhaps, the ability to spend more time with loved ones? Regularly revisiting your financial goals and aligning them with life's milestones infuses purpose and direction into your strategy.

An evolving strategy also demands a keen eye on external trends. The financial landscape is continuously changing, influenced by global economics, technological breakthroughs, and shifting societal norms. Staying informed about these factors helps you make educated decisions, preventing outdated practices from hindering your success. Engage with a community or network that shares insights—whether it's through workshops, discussion groups, or trusted digital platforms. Sharing knowledge amplifies our understanding and illuminates paths we might not traverse alone.

Financial growth isn't a solo venture. Embrace input from mentors, financial advisors, and insightful peers to broaden your perspective. Financially savvy advice can sometimes stem from an unexpected source. Listening to diverse opinions fosters a strategy enriched by the wisdom and experience of others, mitigating blind spots and fortifying your financial foundation.

Mindfulness and reflection should be integral to your strategy. Regular financial check-ins are akin to tending a garden: periodically stepping back to assess progress, celebrate growth, and envision where you want to head next. Pose questions that challenge the status quo: Are my investments aligned with my tolerance for risk? Am I putting too much emphasis on short-term gains at the expense of long-term stability? These reflections guide necessary tweaks and shifts.

Moreover, minimalism plays a vital role in this evolution. Stripping away complexities enables you to see what's essential. Think of it as decluttering your financial garden to allow the healthiest plants to flourish. Reevaluate subscriptions, expenses, and even investment vehicles that no longer contribute to your financial wellbeing. Simplification isn't about deprivation; it's about clarity and focus, setting the stage for sustainable growth. Finally, evolve your financial strategy with authenticity. Ensure that each decision resonates with your core values. This authenticity is the bedrock of contentment, turning financial freedom into a lived experience rather than a distant goal. As you navigate this journey, remember that adaptation is a natural and necessary part of life. By embracing change with intention and joy, you craft a financial strategy that is not only robust and resilient but truly your own.

Chapter 24: Reflecting and Reinventing

In our journey towards financial freedom and simplicity, pausing to reflect becomes indispensable. It's a chance to look back on the path we have carved, taking note of lessons learned and successes reached. Think about the moments that brought the most peace and the decisions that sparked unnecessary stress. This reflection isn't just about seesawing through past actions but understanding the intricate dance between our financial choices and personal growth.

This moment of reflection naturally segues into the art of reinventing ourselves. Just as nature continuously adapts, we too must be willing to pivot and adjust our approaches as necessary. Our initial strategies may have set the direction, but life's unpredictability requires us to refine and sometimes overhaul our plans. This isn't about erasing what you've done but building upon a framework that allows for resilience and flexibility in the face of change. This process is about staying true to your minimalist principles while remaining open to new perspectives.

Regular financial assessments are crucial in this phase. These evaluations aren't merely for tracking numbers; they allow us to realign our trajectory with our long-term goals and values. Consider setting aside dedicated time each month or quarter to review your financial status, asking critical questions: Are your investments still aligned with your risk tolerance? Is your spending reflecting your core values? By doing so, you'll not only stay the course but discern new paths when the old ones no longer serve you.

As you continue to navigate through various life stages, remember that minimalism, at its core, is a dynamic process. Adapting it over time means acknowledging that your needs and circumstances evolve. Embrace these changes with courage and clarity. Reinvention doesn't happen overnight. It's the result of incremental choices that, over time, yield profound transformations.

This chapter, thus, becomes a testament to the power of reflective adaptation—encouraging an ever-evolving connection to our financial and personal landscapes with intention and integrity.

Regular Financial Assessments

Regular financial assessments are not just a task to check off your to-do list. They are the compass directing you through the uncharted waters of your financial journey. Each assessment is a moment to pause, reflect, and evaluate your position relative to your goals. When you engage in financial assessments, it's a celebration of your past successes, an acknowledgment of missteps, and a strategic session for future outcomes.

Financial assessments begin with the simple question: "Where am I now?" This involves a meticulous look at your current financial standing. It's a mosaic constructed from pieces like income, savings, debts, and investments. Once you have a comprehensive picture, you can sense what's working and pinpoint the areas in need of adjustment. Remember, this analysis isn't about self-criticism—it's a launchpad for growth. It's about understanding that even small, consistent changes can lead to significant improvements.

Creating a habit of regular financial assessments requires discipline, much like the way a gardener tends to their plants. You may start by designating a specific day each month to sit down and review your financial documents. Whether it's the last Sunday of the month or a quiet Tuesday morning, make it a ritual. As you review, take notes of changes in your expenditures or any unexpected financial windfalls or shortfalls. Documenting these insights creates a historical record, a tool you can use to recognize patterns and make informed decisions.

As your financial goals evolve, so too should your assessment process. For those just starting out, focus might be on understanding where every dollar goes. For someone more seasoned on this journey, it might involve fine-tuning an investment portfolio or contemplating early retirement scenarios. The key is adaptability; a financial assessment should never be stagnant. It should morph with your financial landscape, echoing your aspirations and responding to life's inevitable twists and turns.

These assessments are also a time to evaluate whether your spending aligns with your values—a core tenet of minimalist living. Ask yourself: Are these expenses enriching your life, or are they relics of an old way of thinking? Maybe that gym membership serves as a crucial outlet for mental health, or perhaps it's a monthly deduction with the weight of obligation. Use these moments to re-align your spending with your current priorities, granting yourself permission to prune what no longer serves you.

Consider involving a trusted partner in your financial reflections. Whether it's a spouse, friend, or financial advisor, another perspective can shine a light on blind spots or overlooked opportunities. Collaborative assessment can foster accountability and create a shared commitment to financial objectives. Discussing finances, when approached openly, strengthens relationships and can transform finances from a source of stress into a shared journey toward growth.

It's crucial during these assessments to not only gaze inward at numbers and charts but outward at the ever-changing economic environment. The markets ebb and flow, policies shift, and new technologies emerge. Regular financial assessments equip you to adapt to these changes. The knowledge you gather empowers you to turn potential threats into opportunities—aligning your strategy with the broader world rather than being swept along by its currents.

In these moments of reflection, also focus on celebrating victories. Did you manage to stick to a budget this month? Was there a debt that's finally off your books? Did savings goals boost your sense of security? Celebrate these wins, no matter how small they may seem. Transforming financial assessments into a process of self-affirmation cultivates positivity and motivates you to keep moving forward.

Let's not ignore the unexpected elements assessments can reveal. Sometimes you uncover trends that signify a need for more substantial life changes—perhaps a career shift to align better with financial goals or reconsideration of long-term plans. These revelations can be daunting, but they also hold the promise of reinvention. By staying informed and flexible, you open up pathways to reinvent not just your finances but your lifestyle as a whole.

Ultimately, regular financial assessments are an empowering practice. They ground your financial journey in reality, steering you away from fantasies and towards pragmatic steps that materialize your dreams. By consistently engaging in this practice, simplicity and wealth no longer become distant ideals but intertwined realities. With discipline and clarity, the path to financial freedom and intentional living begins to become less about chance and more about choice.

Adapting Minimalism Over Time

Embracing minimalism isn't just a one-time event; it's an evolving journey that adapts to the rhythms of life. As you step into this world focused on intentionality and simplicity, understand that it's as much about living with purpose as it is about living with less. Just like your needs and circumstances change, so too should your minimalist lifestyle. The essence of minimalism lies in its flexibility, making it a living, breathing concept that grows alongside you.

Starting out, you may have zealously decluttered and simplified your physical spaces, motivated by the promise of mental clarity and freedom. But as time wears on, you might find yourself facing new challenges and shifting priorities. It's important to realize that adaptation is not a sign of failure but a beacon of growth. As your life evolves, your minimalist practices can morph to support your new goals and dreams.

Consider the foundational principles of minimalism. While it's about reducing, it also emphasizes enhancing the quality of what remains. As you move through different stages of life, redefine what "essential" means to you. In your early stages, it might have meant paring down your wardrobe to only the outfits you love and wear frequently. Later, it could mean focusing on experiences over possessions, spending time in nature, or building deep, meaningful connections with others.

Your financial context is another area where minimalism can adaptively flourish. Just as you streamlined your home, look at your financial portfolio with a fresh perspective. Early on, your focus might be on aggressively paying down debt or creating a solid emergency fund. As you achieve these milestones, pivot toward investing wisely for long-term wealth. Be open to reallocating resources in a way that serves your current needs and future aspirations. Simplicity doesn't mean rigidity—it's adaptability that ensures sustained success.

Every new chapter in your life invites a reexamination of what truly matters. Think about transitions like changing jobs, growing a family, or preparing for retirement. Each brings a new lens through which to evaluate your minimalist goals. The art of adapting your minimalist approach begins with these transitions, ensuring that your financial and personal choices are aligned with your evolving perception of value and purpose.

Set regular intervals to reflect on what minimalism means to you. Like tending a garden, what you nurture may vary depending on the season. In this chapter of reinvention, give yourself the permission to prune, plant, and relish in the notion of a life that's uncluttered yet full of richness. Discovery lies not in having everything, but in appreciating the beauty of what you deliberately choose.

And don't forget, minimalism isn't just about what you discard—it's about what you keep. It calls for a commitment to invest deeply in fewer, more meaningful aspects of your life. This could mean deepening your skills in a hobby that brings you joy or committing to a healthier lifestyle that ensures both physical well-being and financial savings in the long run. By doing so, you embrace a minimalist approach that continues to offer greater returns, both personally and financially.

Embracing the dynamism of minimalism also requires awareness of external influences. Social pressures can ebb and flow, demanding that you flatten your desires anew in pursuit of an authentic life. But instead of yielding, challenge these pressures by recommitting to your values, seeing them as opportunities to strengthen your minimalist philosophy rather than obstacles. Strong boundaries and a clear sense of purpose can guide you through these shifts.

Communication also plays a critical role in this continual adaptation. Keeping open dialogues with those closest to you ensures that your minimalist journey unfolds in harmony with your relationships. Discussing shared goals, aligning your visions of simplicity, and supporting each other's growth and introspection can transform your minimalist pursuits from a solitary journey into a collaborative, supportive lifestyle.

Ultimately, the magic of minimalism lies in its profound simplicity coupled with its powerful adaptability. Life will continue to present its waves of change. Your challenge—and your opportunity—is to ride those waves with a minimalist outlook, constantly adjusting and refining as you go. This living approach to minimalism not only helps simplify your financial life but enriches your journey toward sustained wealth and intentional living.

As you embrace the fluidity of minimalism, you'll find a sustainable rhythm that speaks to the heart of who you are. Flexibility becomes your ally, allowing you to navigate life's uncertainties with grace and grit. Through adaptation, you'll discover the true essence of minimalism: a potent enabler of growth that ensures your journey remains deeply personal and profoundly fulfilling.

Chapter 25: Leaving a Minimalist Legacy

As you stand on the brink of tomorrow, the impact of your minimalist journey begins to ripple outward. You've sifted through your life, retaining only what's necessary, and now it's time to think about what you leave behind. It's more than just passing down wealth; it's about imparting values that prioritize simplicity and sustainability. Your legacy is a beacon of how intentional living can shape both material and spiritual prosperity for generations to come.

Consider the idea of generational wealth as more than just monetary inheritance. Wealth also encompasses knowledge, values, and habits. Encourage those who follow in your footsteps to embrace the principles of minimalism. Teach them the art of finding joy in fewer possessions, the power of thoughtful spending, and the freedom that comes with living debt-free. Your actions today create a path for them to navigate the complex world with clarity and purpose.

But it's not solely about those in your family. Inspiring others through your financial journey involves sharing stories of triumphs and trials. Embody the change you wish to see, allowing your minimalist lifestyle to speak volumes without words. Community engagement can be as simple as hosting a workshop or participating in online forums to spread awareness and encourage dialogue around minimalism. Your experiences might provide the spark someone needs to set their own course toward a liberated financial future.

Reflect on the tools and strategies that have served you well. Capture your wisdom in a journal or digital format for others to reference. This collection of insights and lessons becomes a treasure trove for future generations, offering guidance and motivation. By curating a repository of your journey, you're not just leaving behind a legacy of financial freedom but also an enduring testament to the power of thoughtful living.

Planning for Generational Wealth

In the journey of adopting a minimalist lifestyle, planning for generational wealth isn't just an aspirational objective—it's a solemn commitment to those who follow in our footsteps. This isn't about hoarding wealth but rather about creating a sustainable financial environment where simplicity and abundance coexist harmoniously. To leave a meaningful financial legacy, it's essential to understand that generational wealth is profoundly linked with stewardship. It's about nurturing what we have been given and empowering the next generation with tools, values, and success benchmarks that transcend mere monetary inheritance.

Generational wealth starts with education. Teaching children the value of money, how to manage it wisely, and the power of living with less are foundational lessons that can lead to financial literacy and independence. These skills aren't just taught through words; they're imparted through actions and the everyday decisions we make. When we choose experiences over possessions or commit to mindful purchases, we're modeling financial behaviors that can last a lifetime. These lessons form the building blocks of a resilient and financially aware generation that understands the worth of simplicity and intentionality.

Developing a financial plan that caters to future generations requires a shift in perspective. Instead of focusing solely on accumulating wealth, consider how this wealth will be distributed and used for the greater good of family and community. You might ask, what kind of financial world do we want to leave for the ones after us? Crafting an estate plan that reflects personal values is critical—be it through trusts, investments in sustainable ventures, or donations to causes that resonate deeply with personal beliefs. An estate plan should be a reflection of what matters most, balancing the needs of loved ones with the impact we wish to have on the world.

Open communication about finances can prevent misunderstandings and foster a culture of transparency and mutual respect. Share your approach to minimalist living with family members, and involve them in financial discussions. This inclusion not only demystifies financial management but also cultivates a shared sense of responsibility. When everyone understands the intention behind financial decisions, they are more likely to respect and emulate these practices. This is particularly important for the younger generation, who learn best through inclusion and participation.

Passing on wealth also involves passing on the story of how that wealth was acquired. Family stories about perseverance, frugality, and wise investment can serve as cautionary tales or as inspirations that help future generations navigate their own financial journeys. These stories are priceless; they offer context and knowledge that goes beyond numbers and balances. By intertwining these narratives with financial education, you're not just handing over wealth—you're offering insight into how to cultivate it, cherish it, and use it responsibly.

Investments that align with minimalist values focus on quality over quantity. Choose assets that possess both enduring value and the potential for growth. This could mean focusing on real estate, investing in education, or supporting businesses that are committed to sustainability. With the rising awareness of ecological concerns, it's becoming increasingly important to make investments that reflect long-term thinking, rather than short-term gains. Aligning your investment strategy with these values ensures that your financial legacy supports not just future family members, but also the wellbeing of the planet.

Continual learning and adaptation are key components of a generational wealth plan. By keeping abreast of the latest financial trends and challenging the status quo, you ensure that wealth management remains effective and relevant. Encourage family members to seek education, mentorship, and professional advice as tools for maintaining financial health. Emphasizing lifelong learning not only enhances financial acumen but inspires adaptability in the face of economic changes. Resources that enable family members to engage in this continuous learning are as vital as the financial assets themselves.

A legacy built on minimalist principles is inherently different from one that simply focuses on financial gains. It values human connection, shared experiences, and the tranquility that comes from living with intention. By planning for generational wealth through a minimalist lens, we encourage the next generation to find prosperity not just in financial measures, but in relationships, wellbeing, and a sense of purpose. This holistic approach ensures that wealth brings joy and meaning, rather than stress and discord.

Lastly, inspiring others through your financial journey lays the groundwork for collective empowerment. Communities can thrive when individuals share their insights, failures, and triumphs openly. When family members and neighbors see how minimalist living has enhanced your life and legacy, they too can be inspired to reevaluate their financial trajectories. The ripple effect created by such inspiration can lead to greater societal change where financial abundance is accessible and nurtured by all.

By approaching generational wealth with intention and simplicity, we not only secure the financial future of our descendants but also craft a narrative that's rich in purpose. Let's build these legacies not merely on the solid foundation of financial resources but on the pillars of education, communication, sustainability, and community empowerment.

Inspiring Others Through Your Financial Journey

Inspiring others through your financial journey begins with living out your values and letting others see the positive impacts. It's about quietly leading by example rather than preaching from a pulpit. Imagine walking a path so rare yet simple that others can't help but take notice. By adopting minimalist principles, you shine a light on what's possible when financial freedom is approached with clarity and intention. People are naturally curious; they want to know the secret behind someone who's able to maintain joy and abundance without constant financial worry. This is your opportunity to share your journey, not just through words but through the lifestyle you embody.

Minimalism isn't just about living with less; it's about making room for more of what truly matters. When people see you living a life enriched by purpose and financial stability, that influence can be profound. They might notice how you don't stress over money or how you joyfully prioritize experiences over material possessions. This lifestyle can become infectious—not because you're selling a concept but because the conviction and peace it brings are undeniable. Others will inquire and before long, your example can become a lighthouse guiding others to their own financial awakening.

Sharing your story doesn't mean you must have a polished financial narrative. Authenticity is what resonates most. Confess the hurdles you've overcome and the mistakes that taught you valuable lessons. When you talk about your transition to a minimalist financial approach, include the human elements—how it feels to let go of old spending habits or the relief of unburdening yourself from debt. People are drawn to stories that reflect their own struggles, but with an aspirational twist. When they see someone who has managed to find freedom, despite challenges, it inspires them to believe they can do the same.

Sometimes, inspiration comes through simple conversations. It can be sharing a cup of coffee with a colleague or engaging in a casual chat over dinner with friends. In these moments, guide the conversation towards the philosophies that have shaped your financial life. Avoid overwhelming statistics or unsolicited advice; instead, focus on the narratives and experiences that paint a vivid picture of the benefits and peace that come with living minimally. People respond more to the journey than just the destination.

Consider documenting your journey in creative ways that feel genuine to you. Whether it's through a blog, social media posts, or even a video diary, the medium isn't as important as the message itself. Think of these as modern forms of storytelling where you can openly reflect on how minimalist living aligns with your financial goals. This documentation not only serves as inspiration for others but also holds you accountable, continually pushing you forward on your path.

To extend your influence further, think about volunteering your time or expertise in community workshops or financial literacy programs. Schools, community centers, and local organizations are often looking for people to share practical financial advice. By teaching others about minimalism and its financial benefits, you're spreading the seeds of change. Such initiatives allow you to offer tangible guidance, potentially altering the financial trajectories of those you teach.

Never underestimate the power of a close-knit community. Engage with like-minded individuals—those who are either on the same path or aspire to be. Sharing your journey with this community stimulates energy and creativity. Attend minimalist meet-ups or join online forums where you can exchange stories and strategies. These interactions might even bring new insights to refine your financial journey further. Naturally, collaboration, rather than competition, fosters an environment of growth for everyone involved.

Kids often pick up on the lifestyle choices of adults around them. By setting an example of financial minimalism, you empower the next generation to value experiences over things. Involve them in discussions about finances in an age-appropriate way. A family conversation about saving for a shared experience, rather than purchasing more toys, can be a microcosm of larger financial principles. Cultivating these values early on ensures the legacy you're creating extends beyond monetary wealth to include lifelong lessons in intentional and purposeful living.

As you navigate your journey, remember that inspiring others is not about having all the answers. It's about sharing what you've learned and encouraging others to embark on their paths. Your story doesn't need to be perfect; it just needs to be genuine. The humility in sharing both your triumphs and your missteps makes you more relatable. As you radiate the satisfaction that comes with a minimalist approach to wealth, you inevitably become a beacon of change, encouraging others to reevaluate and perhaps simplify their own financial lives in pursuit of true freedom.

Conclusion

As we stand at the end of this journey toward financial freedom and intentional living, it's essential to reflect on the path we've not only contemplated but also embarked upon. Stripping away excess and approaching life with clarity isn't just a strategy—it's a transformative process that invites us to rethink how we live, spend, and grow. This transformation is not about deprivation but about liberation, the freedom found in knowing what's truly essential, and the peace that comes with that insight.

The pursuit of financial simplicity is a compelling call to action that asks us to challenge conventional norms. By embracing minimalism, we shape not just our financial landscape but the very foundation of our lives. This lifestyle encourages us to choose quality over quantity, essence over material, and intentionality over impulse. Each decision becomes a stitch in the fabric of our existence, contributing to a life well-lived, aligned with our deepest values, and sound financial health.

We've explored the power of a minimalist mindset in nurturing wealth and identified the steps to declutter our financial lives. It's about more than paring down our expenses or maintaining a simple budget—though those things are important. It's finding the balance that allows us to freely prioritize what truly matters, including the freedom to pivot when life doesn't go as planned. This adaptability is a crucial aspect of ensuring that our financial goals and personal values remain in sync, providing an anchor in the ever-shifting currents of life.

Building wealth through intentional living involves more than basic financial acumen; it requires a shift in perspective. Viewing money as a tool, not a goal, redefines our relationship with it. By recognizing our financial levers—spending, saving, and investing—we can better appreciate how they work in tandem to sustain a life of purpose and satisfaction. This journey teaches us that financial freedom isn't marked by the digits on a bank statement but by the peace of mind and choices it allows us to enjoy.

Ultimately, this book emphasizes that financial stability and contentment are intertwined with our mindset, attitudes, and daily choices. In inviting simplicity into our lives, we embrace a philosophy that treasures experiences over possessions, resilience over security, and connection over isolation. We've seen how critical this approach is not only for individuals but for families and communities. A legacy of minimalism inspires future generations to value purpose and well-being over accumulation and status.

As these concepts settle into our ethos, they proliferate into every facet of our lives. Simplifying our homes, travel, digital presence, and even our relationships with others reflects a broader commitment to intentional living. Here, personal discovery and growth intersect with environmental and economic sustainability. In practice, this means continuously learning, adapting, and pushing the boundaries of what's possible as agile stewards of our resources and champions of enduring values.

It's vital to realize that this journey requires ongoing reflection and adjustment. Our financial strategies and minimalist principles must evolve with life's changes while providing the flexibility to flourish amidst uncertainty. Through introspection and consistent reevaluation, we can ensure our journey remains authentic and aligned with our purpose. In doing so, we are empowered to navigate challenges with resilience and to seize opportunities as they arise.

Let us carry these learnings forward with courage and conviction, knowing that we've equipped ourselves with the understanding and tools necessary to live a life beyond the bounds of societal pressures and consumerist constraints. We've seen our potential to inspire others, urging them toward a path of financial enlightenment and fulfillment—a legacy that echoes well into the future.

Concluding this exploration doesn't mark an end but a new beginning. It's a commitment to foster a lifestyle that resonates deeply and shared wisdom that illuminates others' paths. As you go forth, remember that simplifying your financial life is not a destination but a living practice—a continuous commitment to create the life you envision, one intentional choice at a time.

Appendix A: Appendix

As you journey toward financial freedom through minimalism, it's essential to have practical and inspiring resources at your fingertips. This appendix aims to offer additional guidance, resources, and tools that complement the strategies discussed throughout the book. Here, you'll find a mix of actionable tips and motivational insights designed to support your endeavors in achieving a financially simplified and intentional lifestyle.

1. Recommended Tools and Resources

- Budgeting Apps: Explore user-friendly tools that help streamline your financial tracking and budgeting process. Look for apps that provide customizable features to align with your minimalist budget.
- Books and Blogs: Dive into literature and blogs that delve deeper into minimalist living and financial independence. These resources might offer new perspectives or reinforce the principles already shared in this book.
- Community Groups: Join online or local communities dedicated to minimalism and financial well-being. Engaging with like-minded individuals can provide support, accountability, and fresh ideas.

2. Inspirational Practices

- Daily Gratitude Journaling: Foster a grateful financial perspective by dedicating a few minutes each day to reflect on what you have, helping to cultivate contentment.
- Regular Financial Check-ins: Schedule consistent times to review your finances, allowing for reflection and adjustment. This practice ensures you're on track to meet your goals and can adapt as needed.
- Simplification Challenges: Periodically challenge yourself to declutter a part of your life, whether it's your closet or your schedule. These challenges can act as refreshing resets to your minimalist journey.

3. Motivational Quotes

Infusing your day with inspiration can sustain your minimalist and financial motivations. Here are a few empowering quotes to keep in mind:

- "Simplicity is the ultimate sophistication."
- "Less is more."
- "It's not the man who has too little, but the man who craves more, that is poor."

4. Continual Learning and Adaptation

The landscape of finance and minimalism evolves over time. Staying informed ensures your strategies remain effective and relevant. Consider engaging in courses, webinars, or finding mentors who align with your minimalist values and financial goals.

This appendix is just the beginning of your ongoing journey to a more simplified and financially free life. We hope these resources and practices empower you to continually strive for the harmonious balance of financial stability and minimalist living.

act-compliance